John Kimberley

Lord Kimberley's defence of the government brothel system

at Hong Kong

John Kimberley

Lord Kimberley's defence of the government brothel system at Hong Kong

ISBN/EAN: 9783337153892

Printed in Europe, USA, Canada, Australia, Japan

Cover: Foto ©Andreas Hilbeck / pixelio.de

More available books at **www.hansebooks.com**

LORD KIMBERLEY'S DEFENCE

OF THE

GOVERNMENT BROTHEL SYSTEM

AT

HONG KONG.

"CORRESPONDENCE RELATING TO THE CONTAGIOUS DISEASES ORDINANCES IN HONG KONG."

(PRESENTED TO BOTH HOUSES OF PARLIAMENT IN AUGUST, 1881.)

WITH AN INTRODUCTION BY THE RT. HON.

JAMES STANSFELD, M.P.

PUBLISHED BY THE

NATIONAL ASSOCIATION FOR THE REPEAL OF THE CONTAGIOUS DISEASES ACTS,

2, WESTMINSTER CHAMBERS, LONDON, S.W.

To be had of the Secretary, price Sixpence, post-free.

1882.

INTRODUCTION.

TO THE READER.

I INVITE a very careful perusal of the following pages, for the general accuracy of whose contents I am willing to hold myself responsible.

In my opinion the correspondence must be held to modify the rightful attitude and duty of "Repealers" who are "Liberals" towards Her Majesty's Government.

They have nothing to hope from any Government of whose views Lord Kimberley's letter of July 26, 1881, is a deliberate exposition, put forward whilst a Committee of the House is still inquiring into the principles and operation of the English Contagious Diseases Acts.

I shall take the earliest practicable opportunity of challenging this declaration of policy and principle in the House of Commons.

J. STANSFELD.

Stoke Lodge, Hyde Park Gate,

London, S.W.,

Jan. 18, 1882.

LORD KIMBERLEY'S DEFENCE OF THE GOVERNMENT BROTHEL SYSTEM AT HONG KONG.

"CORRESPONDENCE RELATING TO THE CONTAGIOUS DISEASES ORDINANCES IN HONG KONG."

(Presented to both Houses of Parliament in August, 1881.)

In the course of the Session of 1880, the Right Hon. J. Stansfeld, M.P., asked for the production of this Correspondence and was answered that it should be "presented by command" when concluded. It has now been presented and it concludes with the letter of Lord Kimberley to the Governor of Hong Kong, Sir J. Pope Hennessey, of June 26th, 1881, which is reprinted in the following pages.

In the year 1877 Sir J. Pope Hennessey appointed a Commission of Inquiry into the working of the Contagious Diseases Ordinances in Hong Kong. Mr. Stansfeld asked for copies of their report and of the evidence taken before them. Sir Michael Hicks Beach consented to place on the table the report, but not the evidence. It so happened, however, that both the evidence and the report had been forwarded to Mr. Stansfeld by the Governor of Hong Kong,* and Mr. Stansfeld placed both in the hands of the National Association for the repeal of the Contagious Diseases Acts, who published a summary of the information therein contained in the columns of their organ, *The Shield*, which summary was subsequently reprinted for distribution in pamphlet form.

Briefly stated, the circumstances which induced the Governor of Hong Kong to appoint the Commission of Inquiry, were as follows:—
An inquest was held, Oct. 17, 1877, at the Goverment Civil Hospital,

---

* For which Act the Governor was severely taken to task by the Home Government. See Appendix (A.)

Hong Kong, upon the bodies of two Chinese women, who were killed by falling from the roof of a house, whither they had fled in the attempt to escape from the police, who had broken into the house on the ground that it was an "unlicensed" brothel. The coroner's jury, having certified the cause of the death of the women, appended to their verdict a recommendation "that the whole system of obtaining convictions against unlicensed brothels be thoroughly revised, as the present practice is, in their opinion, both illegal and immoral."

The first letter in this important Correspondence is from the Governor of Hong Kong, Sir J. Pope Hennessey, to Lord Carnarvon (Nov. 1, 1877), forwarding the local papers containing a full report of the inquest on the two Chinese women, and calling attention to the recommendation of the coroner's jury. Sir J. P. Hennessey adds, "I have taken the responsibility of putting a stop to a practice which has existed in this Colony since September, 1868,* when Sir Richard MacDonnell sanctioned *the appropriation of Government money for the pay of informers who might induce Chinese women to prostitute themselves and thus bring them under the penal clauses of the Contagious Diseases Ordinance†.* . . . I had no idea that the Secret Service Fund was used for this loathsome purpose until my attention was drawn to an inquest on the bodies of two Chinese women who were killed by falling from a house in which one of the informers employed by the Registrar-General was pursuing his avocations."

It may, at first sight, appear incredible that any Government should systematically employ one class of the community to bribe another class to commit prostitution in order that they might incur punishment at the hands of the State, but full details of the

---

* There is, apparently, some error here as to date. The Commissioners state in their Report (page 10): "In this year (1860) the services of informers were first resorted to," and they quote instances in which an inspector and various police constables acted in that capacity in plain clothes. It would seem that the practice was illegally carried on until it was sanctioned by Sir R. MacDonnell in 1868 after the passing of Ordinance 10 of 1867.

† The Italics, throughout this pamphlet, are our own.

purpose of the Government in so acting and of the results of their action will be found in the official Report of the Commission nominated by the Governor of Hong Kong to inquire into the subject and the evidence thereunto appended. (House of Commons' paper, No. 118, in 1880.)

From that evidence it appears that until the date of Governor Hennessey's letter to Lord Carnarvon, quoted above, the Registrar-General of Hong Kong had been in the habit of employing " Europeans, soldiers, sailors, English members of the spy-police, employés of the Naval Yard, inferior employés of the Registrar General's Department, and the lowest class of Chinamen " to bribe Chinese women to commit prostitution in their own dwelling house or room. These informers were provided with money* for the purpose, in the form of dollar notes which were previously marked by the inspectors of the spy-police, in order that the subsequent finding of those notes in the accused woman's possession, or in her apartment, might be used as evidence in support of the informer's assertion that he had accomplished the task set before him by the representatives of the Government, and thus enable the Inspectors to arrest her.†

The Report of the Hong Kong Commission, the evidence brought before that Commission and the official correspondence now before us, between the Governor of Hong Kong and the Home Government, clear up all that might have remained obscure as to the motives which could induce the representatives of the English Government to bribe Chinese women to commit prostitution for the sole apparent aim of punishing them for so doing.

The purpose of the Officials is two-fold:

In the first place we learn from these documents that the Government has assumed to itself the sole right to trade in

---

* The Chief Inspector of Brothels, Whitehead, in his evidence said: " My instructions were to use European informers if possible," and it appears from the evidence before the Commission that the informers got from 5 dols. to 10 dols. and 20 dols.

† It is well to note here that the Registrar General whose employées perform these services, is also the JUDGE in the first instance before whom the arrested persons are taken, appeals being made practically impossible. (See Appendix D, Ordinance 10 of 1867).

prostitution in Hong Kong and is Sole Licensor of brothels in that Colony. It derives a considerable income both from the fees received from "licensed" brothels and from the fines levied upon those who carry on the trade of prostitution without purchasing a permit. The Registrar General, whose business it is to license brothels and to collect the revenue derived from prostitution, consequently regards all females who commit prostitution without paying duty to the Government, precisely as the officials who collect other branches of the revenue regard all persons, male or female, who carry on any other trade by contraband. And the Government has reserved to itself the right to levy a duty on the bodies of women in Hong Kong, precisely as it has reserved to itself the right to levy duties upon brandy, tobacco and other profitable articles of consumption; and heavy fines are therefore levied upon those who attempt to defraud the revenue in this branch of commerce.

In the second place, the arrest of the women enabled the officials to store those whose bodies were to be offered for sale, in the Government warehouses—the lawful, licensed brothels—and thereby to secure that the articles offered by them to the public should be periodically inspected and medicated by the surgeons hired by the Government for that purpose; it being held to be obvious that every male person whose custom it was to commit prostitution, would prefer that the bodies of the females purchased by him should be cleansed, licensed and warranted by the State, rather than by a private dealer.

It is to be observed that although all brothels in Hong Kong, whether for the use of the Chinese community or of Europeans, have to be licensed and to pay license duties, the "sanitary clauses" of the Ordinances have been only applied to the brothels used by Europeans, on the ground of the insuperable objection of the Chinese themselves to the system; for we learn, from the correspondence now published, that the population of Hong Kong did not by any means accept the point of view of the Government in respect of the official provision of cleansed, medicated and licensed prostitutes. Governor Hennessey writes to Lord Carnarvon (November 1, 1877) that "the European community are ashamed of the revelations that have been made at the inquest, and amongst the Chinese the practice that has been brought to light is viewed with abhorrence." The Governor also says:—"For many years past this branch of the Registrar General's office has led to grave abuses. It has been a fruitful source of extortion, and, what is far worse, a department of the State, which is supposed to be constituted for the protection* of the Chinese, has been employing a dangerously loose system, whereby the sanctity of native households may be seriously compromised."

It appeared from the evidence given by the police inspectors at the inquest on the Chinese women, that besides the monies entrusted to them "to induce Chinese women to commit prostitution," the informers were well rewarded for their real or professed success in so doing, and that all their "expenses" (wine, suppers, &c., &c.) were paid by the Government. "We were told," said Inspector Lee to the coroner's jury, "to engage men even at five dollars each. We made out the bills, the Registrar General signed them, and they were sent to the Captain Superintendent of Police and paid out of the Secret Service Fund."

On April 4, 1878, Sir Harcourt Johnstone asked the Secretary of State for the Colonies " If he would cause special investigation to be made as to the manner in which the revenue derived from licensing houses of ill-fame was raised and expended for the service of the Colony."

Sir Michael Hicks Beach wrote to Governor Hennessey on April 13, enclosing a copy of the above question and saying, "It has been alleged that the balance of the fund now in hand amounts to 50,000 dols.," and desiring him to obtain information on the subject and report the result to him.

The Governor replied by despatch, "the licenses for prostitutes, &c., bring in a nett profit of about 50,000 dols."

---

* The Governor here alludes to the fact that (as stated by Mr. H. T. Ball, then Acting Attorney General in Hong Kong, in his report on the Contagious Diseases Ordinance of 1867) "by Sec. 4, of Ordinance 8 of 1858, the Registrar General is, by virtue of his office . . . . . the Protector of the Chinese Inhabitants of this Colony." The reader will be enabled by these pages to judge the nature and amount of *protection* afforded by him to the *female* inhabitants of the Colony.

This despatch was followed by a letter (July 1, 1878) in which the Governor explained that " the section of the Contagious Diseases Ordinance, No. 10, of 1867, by which *brothel licenses and fines and fees from prostitutes* were to form a separate fund for the purposes of the Ordinance was not complied with, but such monies were treated as part of the regular revenue and used for the general purposes of Government." The meaning of this appears to be that it had not at first been supposed that the sum realised from " brothel licenses, and fines and fees from prostitutes " would do more than recoup the Government for the expenses incurred by them in their efforts to provide the European inhabitants of Hong Kong with healthy Chinese prostitutes, but that on the discovery that the amount of " nett profits " resulting from the trade in the bodies of Chinese women was so large, the Government took to itself the reward of its solicitude for the satisfaction of the sexual appetites of its male subjects.* The correspondence now before us **reveals** the deep sympathy felt by English officials at home for **the** desires of their countrymen abroad in this matter of prostitution, **and** their unceasing anxiety to surround men who indulge in debauchery with every possible protection, facilitation, comfort and convenience in their power.

On June 20, 1879, Sir Michael Hicks Beach forwarded a copy **of the** Report of the Hong Kong Commission to the **Admiralty** (June 20, 1879), calling their Lordships attention **to the** " system of employing paid informers to discover prostitutes

* In illustration of this solicitude on the part of the Government we may mention that, on the 6th November, 1866, Lord Carnavon wrote to Sir R. MacDonnell, then Governor of Hong Kong, forwarding a copy of the Contagious Diseases Act of that year, saying : " I desire to impress upon you that Her Majesty's Government regard this question as one of great importance, and I wish you take the earliest opportunity of bringing the subject under the consideration of your Legislature *with a view to the enactment of a law founded on the principle of the Imperial Act.* The matter is one which concerns the well-being of those places in which Her Majesty's troops are quartered, scarcely less than the well-being of the troops them. selves, and I am sure that I may calculate on the co-operation of your Government and Legislature *in giving effect to the desires of Her Majesty's Government.*"—Document 23, Appendix to Report of the Hong Kong Commission, p. 218.

in unlicensed houses, the medical examination of women who have been found not to be prostitutes,* the seizing of money in unlicensed houses, and the illegal practice by which the inspectors have arrested women instead of merely issuing summonses to the inmates of such houses." These things Sir Michael Hicks Beach stigmatized as " abuses which should be remedied," but, nevertheless, he required " to be acquainted with their Lordships views " as to these illegal practices against the female inhabitants of a Colony in the government of which he represented the British nation, before taking any steps to put a stop to those abuses, because they " might have a very important bearing on the sanitary condition of Her Majesty's military and naval forces stationed at or visiting Hong Kong."

Their Lordships, in reply (Aug. 5, 1879), " declined to criticize the Ordinances of the Contagious Diseases Act in Hong Kong," but added : " They trust that the Act will be maintained in that Colony where it has proved of so much benefit to her Majesty's Navy." Sir Michael Hicks Beach then requested their Lordships (August 18, 1879) to reconsider their decision not to offer an opinion on the subject, and " to favour him with a Report on the several recommendations of the Colonial Commission from the officer who advises the Board of Admiralty on these matters." Their Lordships consequently forwarded to the Colonial Office (Nov. 13, 1879) a copy of a letter from Mr. W. H. Sloggett, inspector of the hospitals instituted by the Contagious Diseases Acts in England for the inspection and medication of female prostitutes, and of his remarks upon the Report of the Hong Kong Commission.

Reference to the " conclusions and suggestions " of the Report of the Hong Kong Commissioners† will suffice to show that the subject was felt by them to involve points of constitutional law, and they state in the body of their Report, that " the Brothel laws, having been founded on a system of coercion by means of

---

* The Commissioners give many instances in their Report in which women and girls were arrested as prostitutes, sent to hospital, and compelled to undergo the infamous ordeal of inspection by the Government surgeon, and found to be virgins.

† See Appendix B.

fine and imprisonment, their history, in one of its most important divisions has been written in Judicial Records." Moreover, they quote in the appendix, the " most weighty objections urged by the Attorney General, Mr., now Sir Julian Pauncefote, to the policy of *subjecting persons to fine and imprisonment without the safeguards which surround the administration of justice in a public and open court.*" (See appendix to Report of the Hong Kong Commission, Document 27, page 221).

Sir Richard MacDonnell, who was Governor of Hong Kong in 1867, appears to have been highly indignant at Sir Julian Pauncefote's respect for these safeguards of personal freedom. He appended a minute to the Attorney General's memorandum in which he said : ". . . I fail to see much of the applicability of the Attorney General's argument to the question. . . . At all events the experiment of dealing with brothels and their inmates through the magistrates in an open Court has been tried and *failed*. Why should we try it again? Experience has shown that the evidence which is necessary for arriving at conclusions in points connected with the ' Social Evil ' here, *cannot be produced in open Court*. The whole machinery was at a stand-still. I have had indubitable evidence of malpractices, but could not obtain convictions, because I could not get the evidence into open Court, and yet the Attorney-General wishes *to sacrifice the object of the projected legislation*, to some DREAM OF THE NECESSITY FOR MAINTAINING A MAGNA CHARTA PALLADIUM OF LIBERTY for people who do not understand it." (See Appendix to the Report of the Hong Kong Commission, Document 28, p. 222).

The indifference of the Lords of the Admiralty to the judicial and constitutional aspects of the subject was shown by the fact that they appointed Mr. Sloggett to consider and report upon the Report of the Hong Kong Commissioners. Mr. Sloggett is an ex-examining-surgeon, who, until he was appointed inspector of the hospitals in which prostitutes are " prepared for the market," was himself employed to inspect and prepare them. Lord Kimberley has also thought fit to support his defence of the Government brothel system by the opinions of Mr. Sloggett. The action of the Admiralty

and Lord Kimberley's indorsement of it afford further illustration of
our statement that the sole aim of the authorities who framed the
Contagious Diseases Ordinances of Hong Kong and the Contagious Diseases Acts of England is, that of providing for the
heathful and comfortable debauchery of the male subjects of
Queen Victoria. Mr. Sloggett, who had much to do in framing
the "English Acts," and is paid by the English Government
to carry them out, thinks there is nothing like leather.
He "can but repeat" . . . . "that the Colonial
Ordinance should be based on the principles of the Contagious Diseases Act of 1866, and its provisions limited to
the means of applying these most effectually to the prostitutes of
Hong Kong, such modifications only being admitted as the peculiar
habits of the people and the circumstances of the Colony might
render necessary," * and with regard to the non-inspection of
women in the brothels visited only by Chinese men, Mr. Sloggett
thinks "it is to be regretted that the principles of the
Contagious Diseases Act of 1866, viz., the periodical medical
inspection of all common prostitutes and their detention in
hospital when diseased, were not more closely followed out in the
Hong Kong Ordinance of 1867, which is that now in force."†

The "peculiar habits of the people" induced Chinese men
strongly to object to the personal inspection of Chinese women. The
Registrar-General of Hong Kong, Mr. Cecil C. Smith, had stated in a
report to Lord Granville (Jan. 18, 1869) that it "would be impracticable to introduce a system of medical inspection in the brothels for
the use of the Chinese;" that if it were attempted "the whole of
the Chinese brothel-keepers would close their establishments;"
and his successor, Mr. Alfred Lister, also stated in February, 1869,
that "it would involve the Government in a very perplexing and
endless strife with Chinese prejudice." Mr. Sloggett, who obtained his
living by labouring to secure the comfortable debauchery of un-
prejudiced Englishmen at home, shared the anxiety of the

* Sloggett to Secretary of the Admiralty, Oct. 7, 1879.
† Observations on the Report of the Commissioners on the Contagious
Diseases Ordinances of Hong Kong (forwarded with above).

Government that equal comforts should be provided for **them** abroad, and he once more " regrets that in the administration **of** those Ordinances in Hong Kong, greater consideration had not been paid to the opinions of the Imperial Government as evinced in the Contagious Diseases Acts of 1866 and 1869." *

On June 21, 1880, Governor Hennessey wrote to the Secretary of State for the Colonies—Lord Kimberley—on the subject, alluding to " some of the more serious abuses laid bare by the Commission," amongst others to the fact that one of the European informers who were paid " to go about with marked money to get women to prostitute themselves," . . . and who " had **in** this way become diseased, was still, after he had given evidence to that effect, carelessly retained by the Registrar-General as an informer, and that a few days afterwards his evidence was again recorded, showing that *he had been furnished* with *Government money to have connexion with Chinese women when he was* actually *diseased.*" The Governor further called attention to the facts that " European inspectors of brothels who were known to the Registrar General as married men were still employed as informers . . . . that brothels were licensed by the Registrar General and the examination-rooms for prostitutes placed in streets where European clergymen resided and where schools for European girls existed," etc., etc.

On the 23rd June, 1880, Governor Hennessey forwarded to Lord Kimberley a despatch on the subject of brothel slavery in Hong Kong, which for some reason is not printed in the official copy of the correspondence presented to Parliament. It appears that in 1856, Mr. Labouchere said, in a despatch to Governor Bowring, " The Colonial Government has not I think attached sufficient weight to the very grave fact that in a British Colony large numbers of women should be held in practical slavery for the purposes of prostitution and allowed in some cases to perish miserably of disease in the prosecution of this employment, and for the gain of those to whom they suppose themselves to belong. A class of persons who, by no choice of their own, are subjected

---

* Observations on Report.

to such treatment have an urgent claim on the active protection of the Government."

The first Contagious Disease Ordinance for Hong Kong was passed in 1857.* It contained no provision for the protection of women from brothel slavery. It was passed, as Mr. Sloggett tells us,† " owing to the very strong representations made by different naval officers in command on the China Station," and " for checking the spread of venereal diseases." The Home Government and Colonial Government took no steps whatever to mitigate the slavery of the women ; but it will be seen further on that Lord Kimberley gives the Government, who did not carry out Mr. Labouchere's suggestion, credit for the *intention* of doing so when they passed an Ordinance dealing exclusively with another subject. Neither the despatch in which Lord Kimberley asserts this, nor that from the Governor to which it was a reply, is printed in the correspondence, but their contents may be inferred from Governor Hennessey's despatch of the 13th November, 1880, in which the Governor writes :—

" I have the honour to acknowledge the receipt of your Lordship's despatch of the 29th September, 1880,‡ with reference to my despatch of the 23rd June,§ on the subject of brothel slavery in Hong Kong.

" Having quoted an extract from my despatch to the effect that *the existing law against slavery, if properly enforced by the police, should be sufficient to secure the real freedom of the Chinese women referred to,* your Lordship expresses the opinion that I cannot have formed any distinct plan for grappling with this long-standing evil, and that the despatches I have written have reached no further than exposing the abuses connected with the Government brothel system I found here, and especially the employment of informers. I venture, however, to point out to your Lordship that, in addition to the agency mentioned in the extract from my despach, I indicated, in paragraph 5, another source to which the Government would have also to look in dealing

---

* (See Appendix C.) † Observations on Report.
‡ Not printed. § Not printed.

with this subject, that is the co-operation of the leading members of the Chinese community.

"I take some blame to myself for not having stated this more emphatically, as, in fact, upon it depends the possibility of securing any beneficial effect in this important matter quite as much as upon the proper action of the police.

"On receipt of the despatch now under reply, I called for a précis of the recorded views of the leading Chinese, and a statement of what the Chinese society your Lordship had sanctioned in despatch of the 20th May, 1880,* had actually accomplished in this matter, and on receiving this information I shall forward it without delay, when it will, I think, be made clear to your Lordship that a beneficial effect has already been secured *by the action of the leading Chinese residents.*

"On the general question of the Government system of licensing brothels, your Lordship seems to think that I have not sufficiently recognised that the establishment of the system was a police measure, intended to give the Hong Kong Government some hold upon the brothels, in the hope of improving the condition of the inmates, and of checking the odious species of slavery to which they are subjected. *I can, however, assure your Lordship, whatever good intentions may have been entertained and expressed by Her Majesty's Government when the licensing system was established, that it has been worked for a different purpose from that which Mr. Labouchere in 1856, and your Lordship all along would desire.*

"The real purpose of the brothel legislation here has been, in the odious words so often used, the provision of clean Chinese women for the use of the British soldiers and the sailors of the Royal Navy in this Colony. During the three or four years that I have been here, I have received from each succeeding Admiral on the station, and from the various officers in command of the troops, representations respecting the brothel laws, and without a single exception, showing that they considered that the Government system was devised for this end. I found the officials of the

---

* Not printed.

Hong Kong Government, who were entrusted with the working of the system, devoted apparently to that end . . . .

" Speaking with whatever authority may attach to my residence in the Colony and access to the official records, I am bound not to conceal from your Lordship the undoubted fact that, so far from checking this odious species of slavery, the Contagious Diseases Ordinances of 1857 and 1867 undoubtedly intensified it.

" On the other hand, Sir Arthur Kennedy's legislation of 1873 and 1875 was designed to prevent the buying and selling of Chinese women for prostitution, and was to some extent an antidote to the brothel laws. The history of the legislation of 1873 and 1875 is in one respect not unlike that of the recent action taken in Hong Kong to put down kidnapping. Your Lordship is aware that the year before the Chief Justice, Sir John Smale, moved in the matter, the respectable Chinese residents had memorialised me to take further steps to repress kidnapping and the sale of Chinese women for prostitution, and that at their request I appointed a Committee on the subject in 1878. In the same way I find that Sir Arthur Kennedy's legislation of 1873 was to a great extent due to the representations made to him by the Chinese community. This fact appears on the official records of 1872, and it is noticed in the memorial of the Chinese which I transmitted to Sir Michael Hicks Beach on the 23rd of January, 1880.*

"I lose no time in bringing this point particularly to your Lordship's attention, so that Her Majesty's Government may see the early and practical interest taken by the Chinese themselves in this question, and that your Lordship may look forward with confidence to settling it satisfactorily, provided the co-operation of the native gentlemen of the Colony be secured."

Lord Kimberley replied to the above, December 31, 1880, saying, " . . . I request that you will at your earliest convenience furnish me with a statement containing such particulars as will explain how the Contagious Diseases Ordinances of 1857 and 1867 have increased the slavery of the inmates of the brothels."

The Governor answered on the 15th June, 1881, submitting the following considerations in support of the statement he had made : ". . . That under the Ordinance No. 12 of 1857, the evils of brothel slavery were intensified and assumed day after day a graver aspect, would seem to have been the opinion of the Registrar General, Mr. Cecil C. Smith, who, ten years after Mr. Labouchere gave the instructions which your Lordship quotes" (and which were not carried out) " wrote on 2nd November, 1866, as follows :—

" ' There is another matter connected with the brothels, licensed and unlicensed, in Hong Kong, which almost daily assumes a graver aspect. I refer to what is no less than the trafficking in human flesh between the brothel-keepers and the vagabonds of the Colony. Women are bought and sold in nearly every brothel in the place. They are induced by specious pretexts to come to Hong Kong, and then, after they are admitted into the brothels, such a system of espionage is kept over them, and so frightened do they get, as to prevent any application to the police.'

" So far for the Ordinance of 1857.

" As regards Ordinance No. 10 of 1867, there is the testimony of another Registrar General, Mr. A. Lister, who stated before the Commission in 1877, that he does ' not think the new Ordinance had any real effect, or could have had any effect upon the sale of women.'

" Such is indeed the case.

" But there is yet the important question whether or not the condition of a woman, once sold into virtual slavery to the keeper of a licensed brothel, was in any way ameliorated by the Ordinance of 1867. As regards this point I am disposed to say that the Ordinance No. 10 of 1867, by giving larger powers to the Registrar General, and thereby indirectly to the inspectors with whom the practical working of the Ordinance lies, made the condition of the unfortunate women sold to the keeper of a licensed brothel worse than it was before. For, as the experienced police magistrate, Mr. May, stated in 1877 in his evidence before the Commission, ' the licensed brothel-keepers look upon the inspectors as their protectors.' There can be no doubt of the truth of what Mr. Pang Ui-Shang told the same Commission that 'the fact of licensing these brothels gives the keepers a sort of official authority,' and that 'they boast of the protection of the inspectors.' The natural consequence of this is that the unfortunate women, who, on being conveyed into the Colony, bring with them an extraordinary dread of all foreigners, have no courage to seek their freedom, and, as Inspector Lee stated before the Commission, 'if they had complaints would not make them.' *

" Another mode by which the Contagious Diseases Ordinance of † 1867 intensified brothel slavery is to be found in the compulsory medical examination of Chinese women by foreign doctors, a system which has never been applied to the licensed brothels generally in Hong Kong, but only to those licensed for Europeans. Nevertheless, as Governor Sir Richard MacDonnell stated, this compulsory medical examination was kept in reserve for all brothels ' as *a species of penalty* that may be inflicted whenever the expediency of such a measure was decided on.' But this very species of penalty is *one of the means by which keepers of licensed brothels enforce submission on the part of the Chinese women.* Mr. A. Lister, who had been entrusted with the working of this Ordinance, stated before the Commission that ' new women would almost have preferred going to the whipping post,' and that ' the mere threat of sending them to examination was generally sufficient to keep them in order.' Thus also *the keepers, by* threatening to place their houses under medical inspection, *gained power over those women.*

" It is well known that the lot of a prostitute in a brothel in Canton has less of the characteristics of slavery than the condition of a prostitute in a Hong Kong licensed brothel. An intelligent Chinese gentleman lately stated in explanation of this circumstance that the reason why brothel slavery became intensified in Hong Kong was that the prostitutes of Canton are near to their own kith and kin, subject to a civic control that is itself subject to

---

* It is instructive to compare this with Mr. Sloggett's statement to the Committee of the House of Commons with regard to the women subjected to the slavery of the English Contagious Diseases Acts : " These women would complain at once if they were listened to, but they never do."—An. 206, page 11. *House of Commons, Evidence on the Contagious Diseases Acts, Session 1869.*   † (See Appendix D, Ordinance of 1867.)

public opinion, and that the keepers of brothels in Canton have not that semi-governmental character which the *keepers* of brothels here appear to derive *from their licences, the support of the inspectors of brothels, and the power of compulsory medication by foreign doctors.*

"Mr. Cecil C. Smith recorded in 1869 his opinion that, as regards brothel slavery, 'as long as the Chinese fail to assist themselves by giving information on such matters to the police, it seems hard to find a remedy for this evil.' * So far I entirely agree with him. I am happy to add, however, that the Chinese have come forward, and with your Lordship's sanction have established a society for the protection of women and children, which society is now giving the Government valuable assistance in this matter."

To the above extremely conclusive letter, Lord Kimberley replied to Governor Hennessey on July 26, 1881. It will be observed that he throughout assumes that the benevolent intentions of Mr. Labouchero for the protection of women from brothel slavery have been embodied in Ordinances which *contain no single clause or provision touching upon that subject,* and the sanitary and financial provisions of which have been shown by the Governor to have intensified the evil.

Lord Kimberley's letter is as follows :—

"Sir,—I have now the honour to communicate to you the *conclusions†* which I have formed upon the report of the Commission

---

* It is worthy of remark that Mr. Cecil C. Smith, who found it hard to remedy this evil without the assistance of the Chinese, had found it easy for many years to carry on the system which intensifies the evil, in spite of the "abhorrence" with which it was viewed by the Chinese.

† These conclusions appear to be deliberate; they are notified on the 26th June, 1881, and it will be remembered that it was early in the Session of 1880 that Mr. Grant Duff informed Mr. Stansfeld that the correspondence should be placed upon the table by command, as soon as it was concluded. Lord Kimberley states in this letter that his decision was "delayed from various causes, partly in order to obtain the opinion of gentlemen who had experience of the subject in this country." During the whole of this period a Committee of the House of Commons had been sitting on the subject of the English Contagious Diseases Acts, and taking evidence concerning them. Lord Kimberley made no communica-

appointed by you to inquire into the working of the Contagious Diseases Ordinances in Hong Kong. This decision has been delayed from various causes, partly from the bulk of the papers, partly in order to obtain the opinion of gentlemen who have had experience of the subject in this country, and partly owing to the necessity of further communication with yourself in the hope of obtaining from you some practical suggestions for dealing with so-called brothel slavery. I also waited to receive the special report of the Colonial Surgeon upon the condition* of the brothels in 1874, which reached me in your despatch of the 17th of September last. Since that date you have informed me, in your despatch of the 13th November, that the Contagious Diseases Ordinances of 1857 and 1867 have undoubtedly intensified brothel slavery; and in my reply of the 31st December I requested you to furnish me with particulars in explanation of that statement.

"In the first place I request you to convey to the three Commissioners an expression of the thanks of Her Majesty's Government for their services and for the time and labour which they devoted without remuneration to investigating this intricate and unpleasant subject.

"The report of the Commission is a minute and copious document, and throws light upon certain abuses which have arisen in connection with the administration of the Ordinances in question, and which you, as I am glad to acknowledge, have shown every readiness as far as possible to remove.

"I regret, however, that I am unable to accept the conclusions of the report with that full and entire confidence which I should have been glad to bestow upon a document compiled with so much labour.

---

tion to that Committee, and, as far as we are aware, his sole authority is Mr. Sloggett; while, with reference to Mr. Stansfeld, who might be supposed to have some experience upon this subject worthy the consideration of an Ex-Cabinet Colleague, all that Lord Kimberley had to say to the Governor of Hong Kong, who had communicated with Mr. Stansfeld on the subject, was: " I feel it incumbent upon me to point out to you that a Governor is not justified in communicating to *unofficial persons* in this country important documents which have not previously been transmitted by him to the Secretary of State."

* This report treats of the sanitary condition of brothels only.

" The report is that of a majority, **and one of the Commis-sioners** dissents in very important points from his two colleagues.* At the same time, these two latter gentlemen appear to me not to have sufficiently appreciated one of the chief objects *aimed at in these Ordinances*, **and I feel** considerable **difficulty in determining** what amount of **reliance I can safely place upon their recom-mendations,** owing to the omission from the printed † evidence of material documents which deserved equal publicity with the other official records, and **to the want of recognition in** the report (in particulars to which **I will presently allude) of evidence which is** adverse to the views which they recommend for my adoption.

" Their fourth conclusion ‡ is at variance with the opinions of the only European medical men whom they examined, and of the medical authorities of Her Majesty's military and naval forces. No medical or other officer of either branch of Her Majesty's services was called before the Commission, but Dr. Wells and Dr. Grant were asked in writing to express their opinion as to the effect of the Ordinance upon the amount and character of venereal disease, with an intimation that the evidence had left a most unfavourable impression on the minds of the two Commissioners (Mr. Keswick was then absent from the Colony). Both of these gentlemen take a different view from the Commissioners, and a further element of doubt has been introduced by the receipt from the Governor of the Straits Settlements § of a despatch (copy enclosed), from which it appears that a law following the lines of the Hong Kong Ordinance, and affecting, as in Hong Kong, a large Chinese population, is in the Straits Settlements considered to have had eminently satisfactory results.

* With regard to this gentleman's dissent see Appendix E.

† We have already pointed out that Lord Kimberley delayed formulating his conclusions for a whole year. During that time he might have telegraphed for and obtained the material documents in question.

‡ The fourth conclusion of the Commissioners is as follows : " That licensed brothels for foreigners are in themselves sources of infection, and that the evidence before us points to these establishments, rather than to unlicensed houses, as the causes of disease to soldiers and sailors."

§ Is not this Governor Mr. Cecil C. Smith, formerly Registrar General and Licensor of Brothels in Hong Kong?

" The terms of the Commission indicate that the primary object of the investigation was the revision of the method employed in prosecuting unlicensed brothels * ; in other words, the administration of the law having been called in question, the machinery was to be overhauled and a better system introduced. The inquiry, however, developed into a general investigation of the circumstances affecting prostitution in China and in Hong Kong, into the origin of these Ordinances, their effect in regard to kidnapping and ill-treatment of the women by their keepers, their sanitary results, and other cognate matters ; but one vital part of the subject seems to me to have been insufficiently considered, namely, the bearing of these laws upon the great evil of brothel slavery. † Looking to the language of this report, it should have been accompanied by nearly the whole correspondence between the Colony and this office on the subject of both Ordinances. I gather from page 2 of the report that you laid all this correspondence before the Commission ; but, though portions are printed, other material documents are omitted, and it is necessary for the proper comprehension of the difficult questions involved that the whole correspondence should be examined. ‡

" The first page of the report states :—

" ' The shadow of a grave responsibility rests on all who have been

---

* Lord Kimberley is mistaken. The terms of the Commission indicate far more than this. They are as follows :—" It is expedient that certain inquiries and investigations should be made touching the operation of the said Contagious Diseases Ordinance generally, and especially as to the regulations and machinery in force for the suppression of unlicensed brothels."

† The Commissioners had perceived, although Lord Kimberley had not, that the Ordinances contained no clauses in any way touching upon the subject. Moreover the evidence before them proved the truth of the Governor's assertion that their indirect effect was to intensify this " great evil."

‡ The whole of the correspondence between the Colony and the Colonial Office was surely within Lord Kimberley's reach, and if it was necessary to examine it for the proper comprehension of the difficult subject, was it not Lord Kimberley's duty to examine it before arriving at his conclusions, and by publishing all matter in his opinion relevant, but omitted, to give the public the opportunity of doing the same ?

concerned, both in the introduction of this law and in its adminis-tration.

"But we should be flinching from our duty if we allowed it to be thought that, in our judgment, this responsibility stops short with the authorities and officers of this Colony. The law was originally introduced and has been since perpetuated greatly through influences from outside, and in deference to opinions which have not stood the test of experience, and the Ordinance 10 of 1867 received its final sanction when the conclusion arrived at by the Colonial Government was before the Home Authorities, showing that, in the event of the Ordinance becoming law, revenue would be derived from the tainted sources of prostitution among the Chinese, while it had been decided not to enforce against the houses for Chinese only those sanitary clauses' (the medical inspection and treatment of women) 'of the Ordinance which formed its only *raison d'être.*'"

"At page 7 it is said :—

"'Legislation built very much on the lines subsequently followed by Ordinance 10 of 1867, was first applied to the subject of prostitution in this Colony more than 20 years ago. There are certain differences between the Ordinance then passed and the one now in force which we shall presently consider. But the two main principles then adopted prevail to the present day, and may be thus summarised :—

"'1. The legalization of houses of ill-fame in consideration of fees paid to the Government.

"'2. The medical examination of the persons of prostitutes, and their segregation in a Lock hospital for treatment when found diseased.'

"And the Appendix is referred to as containing the most important documents relating to the institution of the Ordinance of 1857.

"Again at page 8, there is this passage :—

"'The object of the Ordinance (1857), *as declared by its preamble,* was strictly limited to making "provisions for checking the spread of venereal diseases within this Colony;" but houses solely for the use of Chinese did not cease to be registered, nor did revenue cease to be derived from them when it became clear that the sanitary clauses of the enactment could never be applied to them. Thus, by indirect means, never apparently contemplated by the Legislature, was Government supervision or control, independent of sanitary reasons, established over a very considerable portion of the prostitution of the place.'

"At page 51 it is said :—

"'The imperative sanitary reasons which formed the ostensible and, indeed, the only admissible ground for establishing governmental relations with brothels, only hold good with respect to less than one-third of the privileged establishments, and the great majority have been allowed to contribute funds year by year towards a sanitary scheme, the benefits of which their inmates have refused practically to partake of.'

"The sixth conclusion, at page 52, in which you express your entire concurrence, states :—

" 'That the Ordinances did not contemplate or justify the licensing and regulation of such houses for purposes other than those connected with the suppression of venereal disease, and that such houses should never have been made a source of revenue.'

" And, at page 53, the report recommends that,—

" ' In future, houses for the sole use of Chinese should not be in any way subject to Government supervision.'

"From these passages it is evident that the framers of the report are of opinion that the Ordinances were enacted chiefly for the purposes of preventing disease and increasing the revenue of the Colony. I shall allude later on to the revenue question, but in order to judge how far a main object was the prevention of disease, the original proposals* on the whole subject must be borne in mind, and I cannot but express my regret for this reason that the full correspondence was not printed with the report. Sir John Bowring's despatch of 2nd of May, 1856, which is not printed, forms, with the reports enclosed in it, an important link in the chain of correspondence, showing how the registration or licensing question arose, and leading up to Mr. Labouchere's reply of 27th August, 1856, which is printed at page 207.†

---

* It is somewhat idle to bear in mind *proposals* which were not judged worthy of being embodied in the Ordinances which are in question, not even in the preamble.

† Lord Kimberley regrets that all the correspondence is not published because it would furnish important links in the chain of evidence as to how Ordinance 12 of 1857 came to be passed. Why does he not quote these important links ? Is it because he forgets or remembers that if *all* the missing links in the chain of evidence consisted of letters urging legislation of a truly protective character, they would prove still more conclusively that the main object of the Government was the prevention of disease, since they finally approved and passed Ordinance 12 of 1857 which, as stated in its preamble, was strictly limited to that main object ; to making provisions for " checking the spread of venereal disease."

" Mr. Labouchere's despatch indicates that he felt that the Colonial Government was not sufficiently impressed with the necessity of protecting the unhappy women who were, and many of whom I fear are still, held in a state of practical slavery; and it authorised the passing of the Draft Ordinance which had been sent home, but *only as a temporary measure until a protective law could be framed and put in force.*

" Sir John Bowring's reply, dated 20th March, 1857, is printed, page 208, but the greater part of its enclosures* are omitted, as well as Mr. Labouchere's reply of 11th August, 1857. It is consequently impossible to gather from the printed documents that Sir John Bowring transmitted two draft Ordinances in this despatch, or that of these the one prepared by Mr. Anstey was merely the previous draft slightly altered, while the other, prepared by Mr. Bridges, and so strongly condemned in Mr. Anstey's letter † which is printed, was in fact preferred by the Secretary of State, and with some modifications became eventually Ordinance No. 12 of 1857. ‡

" Mr. Labouchere writes :—

"' Her Majesty's Government are disposed to prefer the provisions of the Draft Ordinance of Mr Bridges to those of the ' Ordinance for the Repression of certain Diseases.' My despatch of the 27th August last§ will have already explained the grounds of this opinion, and the reasoning there advanced in favour of licensing

---

* Lord Kimberley might have quoted the remainder of the enclosures and the despatch had he believed that they would prove his statement.

† Mr. Chisholm Anstey, then Attorney General of Hong Kong, gave, amongst other reasons for his condemnation of the Draft Ordinance which was adopted by the Government and became Ordinance 12 of 1857, the reasons that " It over-legislates and yet falls short of the purview. It violates the great principle of the law that none shall be forced to self-crimination."

‡ Quite so; and this is the Ordinance, whose title and preamble alike describe it as an Ordinance " For Checking the Spread of Venereal Diseases" within the Colony. We have printed it entire in Appendix C, and it will be found to contain no provisions for the prevention of brothel slavery, or for the protection of "the unhappy women."

§ Not printed. Why did not Lord Kimberley quote it to show " the grounds " on which the second Ordinance was preferred, if those grounds would have proved his case ?

houses of this description only derives additional strength from the great practical difficulty which has evidently attended all attempts at legislation on the principles of mere repression. It appears also that whatever objections of principle may be urged against licensing this class of houses (and I am far from underrating their force) those objections apply with almost or quite equal strength to the provisions of the "Repression" *Ordinance for indemnifying brothel-keepers who act- in conformity with its directions against legal molestation. In either case, *brothels are equally placed under the protection of the law*, though in a different mode and under different conditions.'

"In referring to these passages I have not overlooked the passage at page 44, when, after referring to Mr. Labouchere's despatch of 27th August, 1856, in terms which seem to imply that the idea of registration, as well as of protection, originated with the Secretary of State, which, if intended, is incorrect, the report says :

"' Accordingly we find that, although the brothels set apart for the sole use of Chinese were never subjected to medical supervision, they were kept in all other particulars under the same control as those for the accommodation of foreigners.'

" I have also noted the paragraph which states at page 45,

"' With the internal *cleanliness* and *comfort* of brothels we think the Government has but little to do, but the amelioration of the condition of the inmates is a matter which certainly stands on a different footing, and is one in which the Government has a deep interest ; '

" And that at the foot of page 49 respecting the few cases which

" ' Seem to have any material bearing on the question of the liberty of the women in licensed houses or the amelioration of their condition ; '

" But, after reading these passages, it was with some surprise that I found the report stating at page 51 that

"' Sanitary reasons formed the ostensible, and, indeed, only admissible ground for establishing governmental relations with brothels,'

" And recommending at page 53, that

"' Houses for the sole use of Chinese should not be subject to Government " supervision." '

---

* It will be observed that Mr. Labouchere does not allude to his own proposal that the women should be protected, obviously because that proposal had not been embodied in either of the draft Ordinances in question.

"It is quite clear that Mr. Labouchere, having regard to the unhappy circumstances prevailing in Hong Kong, considered the necessity for the protection of the inmates, as distinguished from their medical treatment, to be a valid reason for giving to the Government supervision and control over all brothels in the Colony.

"Enough appears in the Appendix to indicate that the motives which influenced Mr. Labouchere in 1857 were recognized* in 1867. This view is supported by some parts of Sir R. Mac-donnell's despatch, of 10th August, 1857, the enclosures to which, without the despatch, are printed at pages 218-220 of the Appendix†" (to the Report), "and I notice that the special powers of supervision created in 1857 were continued in 1867 to the Registrar-General, the Superintendent of Police, and persons deputed by them; and these powers are found in a different part of the Ordinance from the provisions relating to medical examination and the duties to be discharged by the medical officers.

"That such was really the case is placed beyond doubt by Sir R. MacDonnell's despatch, of 23rd March, 1868, which contains the following passage:—

"' These police powers of supervision it is *proposed* to exercise at once and continuously for the protection‡ as well of the unfortunate inmates of all licensed houses as others of the same class; and practically the views of Mr. Labouchere, in his despatch of 27th August, 1856, *would* thus be carried out.'

---

* This makes the matter worse, if both in 1857 and 1867 they "recognized" Mr. Labouchere's desire to protect the women only to despise it.

† Not a single line in these enclosures refers to the protection of the inmates of brothels in any shape: the "police supervision" being solely for the purposes of checking venereal disease and securing payment of revenue, and the "protection" afforded being solely the protection of brothel-keepers by the police. As for Sir R. Macdonnell's despatch, Lord Kimberley could have printed it had it borne out his statement. We have printed, above, certain portions of a "minute" by Sir R. Macdonnell, which will show the amount of feeling he had for the liberty of the Chinese women.

‡ It will be seen that it is absolutely untrue that the Ordinance of 1857 created any power of police supervision directed to the protection of the unfortunate inmates of brothels, and that none such were either created or continued by Ordinance 10 of 1867.

"If it be true, as stated at page 46 of the report (though I am not at present convinced upon the point), that Government supervision increases in some respects rather than relieves the servitude of the inmates, as to which, in reply to your despatch of 13th November, 1880, I have called for further explanations, this would form a ground for carefully reviewing and improving the manner in which that supervision is exercised, not for withdrawing it altogether from the houses for Chinese only, which form the great majority of the brothels, and leaving the unhappy inmates to their fate without an attempt at ameliorating their condition ; and I have not failed to observe that Mr. Cecil Smith, in the 17th paragraph of his letter to Sir F. Rogers, printed at page 253 of the Appendix, reports :—

" ' That these instances of virtual slavery exist entirely in the brothels for Chinese, where the women are seen by their own countrymen, and not in the other houses which are frequented by foreigners.'*

" The report, at page 47, states the intention of the Government to have been that the Ordinance of 1857 should be worked with the aid of the whole body of police, but indicates that the then superintendent having set his face against the Ordinance, and not having (to use his own words)

" ' Permitted the police to have anything to do with the control and supervision of brothels under the Ordinance, being apart from the general objects of police duties, and from the great probability of its leading to corruption,'

" it came about that the office of Inspector of Brothels was created, and fell into the hands of inferior men (Rep., pp. 47, 48).

---

* Lord Kimberley forgets to note that Mr. Cecil Smith states in page 3 of the same letter that " although the brothels are practically divided into two classes, yet, except that the inmates of those which are kept apart for Europeans and persons of nationalties other than Chinese are subjected to regular medical inspection, *no difference in the supervision is made*. All the houses are under the immediate control of the Registrar General and his staff, and for the purpose of preventing any breach of the law, are visited continually at all hours both of the day and night." If therefore instances of virtual slavery exist in the brothels for Chinese, the fault must lie with the Registrar-General and his Staff, since such slavery is " a breach of the law," though not of the provisions of the Ordinances. With regard to this matter of virtual slavory, see Appendix F.

"The power of visiting and inspecting registered brothels was, by section 7 of the Ordinance of 1857, vested in the Registrar General (who had some months previously, by Ordinance 6° of 1857, been created Protector of the Chinese) and the chief officers of police ; and it is evident, from the wording of the section, that these powers were distinct, and proceeded† *upon other grounds*

---

* There appears to be some error here. Mr. Henry John Ball, then Acting Attorney-General in Hong Kong, states in his Report on the Contagious Diseases Ordinance of August 9, 1867: that the Protectorship was confered on the Registrar-General by Ordinance 8 of 1858, sec. 4.

† A glance at secs. 7 and 10 of the Ordinance will show the glaring inaccuracy of this reference. It is perfectly monstrous that an English minister should seek to deceive the public by this statement. Having in view the title and preamble as well as the clauses of the Ordinance in question, no lawyer will be found to say that protection of the inmates was within its purview ; whilst it is to be remembered, that Mr. Labouchere himself, in his letter of August 27th, 1856, in which he expresses his desire for the protection of the *inmates* of the brothels from practical slavery, speaks of the forthcoming Ordinance in these words :—" I am not at present prepared to say, and I wish you seriously to consider in what shape and to what extent it is practicable to give this protection. I do not see how it can be given at all till the establishments in which such practices are supposed to exist are brought under the eye, and in some measure under the control of Government. On these grounds, therefore, independently of those which have been pressed upon you by Sir John Stirling and others, I think that these houses of ill-fame and their inmates should be registered and subjected to Police regulations, *in the first instance* of a sanitary character, that a strict medical inspection should be enforced, and that all diseased persons should be removed to hospitals and placed under treatment. The expense of their treatment should be paid either by the public or, if possible, by the persons from whose *control they are taken*, against whom, I will here observe, rather than their unfortunate instruments, the penal provisions of the law should be mainly directed. A law framed on these principles besides the direct effect it would have on the public health, would furnish some *immediate protection* to those who are the first victims of the present system, and would *facilitate such further measures as the Government might deem* it expedient to take hereafter." It will be seen that the whole secret is here. Mr. Labouchere's hope that the law would furnish protection to those who are the first victims of the present system, is appealed to for the purpose of making out a case, although it has never been attempted to realise that hope, and no further measures were ever proposed with that object.

than the sanitary inspection of the women by the medical officers.

"A similar distinction is to be found in the 10th section of the same Ordinance; and these powers of supervising registered houses were again distinct from the provisions relating to the prosecution of unregistered brothels, matters which it was obviously meant should be dealt with by the police in the same manner as other breaches of the statute law.

"The attitude, however, which the police were allowed to adopt towards the Ordinance *appears to me to be one of the causes which frustrated Mr. Labouchere's humane intentions*: and as soon as the object was *thus* lost sight of which induced the Secretary of State to desire that these establishments should be 'under the eye, and in some measure under the control of the Government,' it not unnaturally followed that the special provisions of the Ordinance came to be regarded as little more than machinery for the detection and suppression of unregistered or unlicensed brothels. And as the police, who, I presume, are acquainted with the character of the houses in their several beats, seem to have given little assistance towards the enforcement of the law in these particulars, it is not surprising that the inspectors, whose means of obtaining proofs were likely to be less complete, should have been driven to *extraordinary devices* for procuring evidence in the cases which in the discharge of their duties they found themselves required to bring forward. It seems, indeed, from document No. 32, printed at page 225, that there need have been no difficulty in identifying unlicensed houses, for on that occasion, in 1866, ninety-four were detected in two nights without the aid of the inspector.

"The system of informers paid to obtain evidence by personal intercourse with women, which was introduced in 1868 simultaneously with the appointment of inspectors (p. 10 of Report), was a revolting abuse,[*] which you most properly put a stop to as far back as the month of October, 1877.

"The Commission is dated 12th November, 1877, and the

---

[*] Compare with pages 28 and 29 defending the practice.

28

report December, 1878. It was, therefore, scarcely necessary for the report to have contained so full an analysis of the cases in which this discontinued system had been employed, or the many pages of proceedings in such cases which are printed in the Appendix.

" Turning to the medical side of the subject, I may observe that the report seems to me to pass over somewhat too lightly the horrible circumstances† which gave rise to the discussion which led up to the Ordinance of 1857, and to attach, at least, as much weight to Mr. May's recollection of matters which occurred 20 years before as it does to the official reports written at the time, and not all printed."

[His Lordship here gives details as to disease, upon the authority of Naval and Military officers, to which he thinks the Commissioners did not attach sufficient importance in their report. He then goes on to say :—]

" The severe reprehension which is bestowed in the report on the employment of informers to obtain evidence, and other grave scandals, is well deserved, but the Commissioners in my opinion go too far in their unsparing condemnation of everything connected with the enforcement of the Ordinance. The detection of unlicensed houses was a duty cast upon the Registrar-General and the officers of his department by the provisions of the law, and the obloquy which is cast upon them for their efforts in the discharge of this unpleasant duty appears to me not to be entirely merited. The use of plain clothes (p. 10, 17) seems both proper

---

* We trust that the British Parliament and public will not share this desire of Lord Kimberley that the truth should be concealed. It comes with an ill grace from a Secretary of State who, in the same letter, complains that the Commission have not printed certain correspondence which he could himself produce if he liked, but which he has not chosen to produce. We are not aware of any other instance in which a Commission has been thus publicly rebuked for the publication of evidence which it deemed necessary to elucidate its report.

† These horrible circumstances are simply the usual sensational accounts of disease in the army and navy written by the medical officers of the services.

and natural, considering the services in which the wearers were engaged; and I am not prepared to say that the use of marked money is in itself necessarily reprehensible.* The acceptance of money in consideration of a request for sexual intercourse is evidence of the character of the *recipient* and of the nature of her abode ; and *if* the detective or informer, after giving the money, *leaves the house,*† as appears from the depositions to have been not unfrequently the case, the fact of its acceptance, verified by its discovery in the possession of the alleged recipient, coupled with such other evidence as was forthcoming might be given in proof of the charge. This is quite a separate question

---

* Compare this with page 27, line 3 from bottom, in which his Lordship stigmatizes the system of informers paid to obtain evidence by personal intercourse with women as "a revolting abuse."

† Lord Kimberley does not suggest that informers who do not leave the house should share the punishment inflicted on the women, or even go unrewarded for "the services in which they were engaged." Yet Lord Kimberley has read the Report of the Hong Kong Commissioners, and must have seen their sternly ironical notice of some of these "services" as follows: "It is to be noted, also, that one Hung-A-Wai did, as informer, *with the assistance of public money, and in the interests of justice,* have connexion with a child fifteen years of age (p. 198)," and "(case No. 6,724, p. 185) when Soung-A-Wai slept with Tai-Yau *against her will,* which led to *his* being rewarded, and to her being fined 100 dols., and to the loss of her child." [The wretched victim sold her child to pay the fine.] It will be remembered that the Royal Commissioners on the English Contagious Diseases Acts said in their Report :—"There is no comparison to be made between prostitutes and the men who consort with them. With the one sex the offence is committed as a matter of gain, with the other it is an irregular indulgence of a natural impulse." The evidence of the "cases" which Lord Kimberley thought it "scarcely necessary" to report, sufficiently proves that in most instances the informers did not leave the house without indulging their natural impulses. His Lordship goes farther than the Royal Commissioners, and, apparently thinks that the fact of finding pleasure in a disgusting act, raises the man even when he commits it "for gain" to a position of proud superiority not only over the woman who commits it "for gain," but even over a woman who is *compelled* to submit. See also opinion of Mr. A. Lister, Registrar-General, on the point of the informers leaving the house. (Appendix G.)

from bad faith in the witness, such as is suggested at p. 17, or from the revolting conduct of informers themselves.

" I have read the cases referred to at page 17 of the report, which are selected ' in special illustration of that particular class of prosecutions in which the conviction is obviously based upon the taking of money, which is afterwards found by the inspector upon the woman and matters have gone no further,' and would observe that the receipt of the money is in each case only one of the facts deposed to, and having regard to all the evidence which was given I think it may be open to some doubt† whether it is perfectly clear that the convictions were based on the taking of money.

" The practice of breaking into and arresting the inmates of unlicensed houses led to undoubted abuses, although it seems clear that the inspectors acted under a belief that their proceedings were strictly according to law.

" In these, as in other defects of *administration*, the cause appears to lie in the want of sufficient care in selecting the men actually charged with the working of the Ordinance,‡ and in leaving them too much to themselves when appointed.

---

* In what does the "revolting conduct" consist ? It is not the act of fornication, for the express purpose of the Ordinance Lord Kimberley defends is, to provide opportunities for fornication. It must be that Lord Kimberley considers it " revolting" to commit it otherwhere than in a licensed, Government brothel.

† The Commissioners support their statement by evidence to that effect given by the informers themselves.

‡ Does Lord Kimberley wish the *inspectors* to perform the "services" in which the informers were engaged ? The Commissioners give many examples in their Report of cases in which inspectors and policemen acted as informers. The following are some of these which we give in the words of the Report :—

"1872 . . . The cases in which the inspectors themselves act as detectives find some illustrations deserving notice among the depositions of this year. Case No. 27 (p. 102), in which Horton, *in the discharge of his duty*, 'got into bed' with a Mrs. Cowie, wife of a turnkey in the gaol. . . . Case No. 74 (p. 114) . . . There Horton, having bargained with the first defendant for the deflowering of the second defendant, a child of 15 years of age, arrested them and six others, and the child being taken to the Lock Hospital and subjected to medical examination, proved to be a virgin.

"There was no lack of funds from which to pay thoroughly respectable and trustworthy men* as inspectors, and if they could not be obtained on the spot for the salary offered, the assistance of this office might have been asked for to obtain them from the towns where the Imperial Acts are in force. It is not surprising

". . . . It is noteworthy that in the case (No. 42, p. 164), in which two of the girls arrested proved to be virgins, Inspector Whitehead broke into the house and arrested the women because 'there were reasonable grounds for believing that the house is a brothel.' . . . and that the third and fifth defendants were arrested *because they happened to be in the house*, although, *to the knowledge of Whitehead*, they did not belong to it."

* Lord Kimberley believes what few Englishmen believe, that men who are willing to act as brothel-spies, are likely to remain thoroughly respectable and trustworthy. Mr. C. Vandeleur Creach, Acting Captain Superintendent of Police, said to the Hong Kong Commissioners (An. 239 and 240) :—" I don't think it necessary to give the Inspectors of Brothels the large powers they have. The police would have sufficient powers to carry out the ordinary laws of the Colony as applied to brothels, without any special powers. (Ans. 245 and 246.) If you were to let in the whole force to work Ordinance 10 of 1867, it would ruin the police force by bribery and other temptations. . . . ." Mr. Alfred Lister, Registrar General, who "thinks he heard the very first case under the Ordinance of 1867," says: (An. 89)—". . . . Peterson was my chief inspector . . . . he may have taken bribes." (An. 118.) "Sometimes there was a quarrel at the bottom of an information. I remember such a case with a policeman of the name of McQuade." (An. 126.) "I was always uneasy about my inspectors, because I knew many houses could afford to bribe them." (An. 130.) "The Registrar General is very much dependent on the inspectors, and their temptations are exceptionally great. An inspector might easily double his salary—that is, he could do so without giving rise to suspicions, or without squeezing the people to such an extent as to give rise to complaints. The man whose cupidity was *un-bounded* would soon be found out. The moderate man is more dangerous. . . . ." The importance of the foregoing is increased if taken in conjunction with An. 128 : " In my experience a Chinaman never complains of a policeman till he is in prison. *He is afraid to do so* . . . ." (Aus. 132.) " The whole thing is so demoralising that I don't think you should entrust the whole police force with the working of the Ordinance under any circumstances . . . . If an inspector escapes demoralisation, he does so from his own qualities. It was the greatest blessing for the whole police force to have been free from working the Ordinance. *If demoralisation must take place*, it should be confined to the smallest compass."

that considerable laxity resulted from allowing these men to become independent of police discipline, and to be subject only to the Registrar-General, instead of the details of administration being supervised by means of a daily report of occurrences, such as is made in a police force.

" I agree with the Commissioners in their remarks (Report, p. 28) upon the seizure of marked money if it is beyond doubt that the money taken was detained from the women after it had been used in evidence. The inspectors, however, do not appear to have been questioned on the point, and if the allegation is substantiated by other evidence it has escaped my attention.

" From page 49 of the report it appears that during the ten years in which the Ordinance of 1867 has been in force, the Commissioners can only find 23 cases in all which seem to have any material bearing on the question of the liberty of the women in licensed houses, and the amelioration of their condition.

" In the Appendix however, the following cases which are not mentioned in the Report, nor included in the above 23 cases, will be found to have occurred in the year 1874.*

" No. 4 (Appendix, page 147), where three women successfully applied for assistance against the keeper who had refused to allow them to leave the brothel.

* We have carefully studied the whole of these cases to which Lord Kimberley refers, and we can assert that in no one of them was the liberty of women, in the licensed houses, in the slightest degree affected by the existence of the Contagious Diseases Ordinance. Several of these are cases in which brothel-keepers are fined for " keeping an incorrect list of inmates," i.e.—having omitted to strike off the list, which they are compelled to keep —the names of girls who had quitted the brothel. This they are perfectly free to do, although Lord Kimberley ignores the fact. (See Inspector White-head's evidence, Appendix F., under heading " Brothel Slavery.") The cases in which charges of interference with liberty are made, are, without excep-tion, cases coming under the ordinary law and in the adjustment of them no assistance was rendered by the provisions of the Ordinance. We cannot help thinking that Lord Kimberley would scarcely have referred to them in the way he has done, if he had not known that the evidence accompanying the Report was not accessible to the public and that, therefore, his interpre-tation of those cases, if a mistaken one, was not likely to be called in question. (See also Appendix F.)

" No. 5 (Appendix, page 148), a similar case with one complainant.

" No. 19 (Appendix, page 152), where a keeper detained the property of a girl who wished to leave.

" A case without number, but which apparently should be No. 37 (Appendix, page 160), where several girls were saved from being sent to San Francisco against their will. No. 38 (page 161) where the property of the same girls was in question, and was apparently recovered for them after it had got into improper hands.

" No. 53 (Appendix, page 164), where a woman complained that her grand-daughter who had gone willingly to Singapore had there been sold, on behalf of a Hong Kong creditor, apparently a procuress. In this case nothing could be done by the Registrar-General, beyond binding the woman over; but it instances the working of the Ordinance.

" Also No. 57 (Appendix, page 165), where a girl of weak intellect was rescued when about to be taken to Singapore without her consent.

" These cases and No. 76 of 1871 (Appendix, page 97), and No. 23 of 1873 (Appendix, page 125), neither of which are referred to, and Mr. Whitehead's evidence (Answer 397), that the inmates look upon the Registrar-General as their protector, * and Mr. Creagh's statement† (Answer 238), that with reference to kidnapping and sale of women, no case has *originated* with the Police Force, appear to me to show that the operation of these Ordinances has not been so entirely ineffective in securing the liberty of these wretched women, as the Commissioners appear to consider (Report, page 5). How far their effect may have been to deter the brothel-keepers from attempts to keep women in a state of slavery is necessarily matter of conjecture, but it was the opinion of Mr. Smith in 1869 (Appendix, page 254, par. 17), that cases of virtual‡

---

* The reader will remember that Mr. Whitehead is a policeman, employed as purveyor of women to the Government market; they have seen the Commissioners' statements as to the method by which the supply of prostitutes is recruited for the Government brothels, and they will attach about the same value to Mr. Whithead's evidence on this subject as to Mr. Anniss' assertions with regard to the protection afforded by himself to young girls.

† How the statement of a Superintendent of Police that no case of kidnapping and sale of women has *originated* with the police force, can tend to show that their supervision has been, in any degree effective in securing the liberty of these wretched women, is entirely beyond comprehension.

‡ See Appendix F.

slavery were confined to the houses for Chinese ; and if this be the case it may not unreasonably be inferred that the closer supervision over the houses for foreigners had had some effect in protecting their inmates.

"On the whole, I feel obliged to state as the result of a careful examination of the report testing it by the evidence in the Appendix and in the records of this Department,* that its treatment of questions both of fact and of principle is inconclusive, and I find myself therefore placed in a position of some embarrassment, since, in the despatch† transmitting it, you merely express your entire concurrence in its conclusions, accompanying it with no explanations on your own part, and with no opinion as to the manner in which the machinery of the Ordinance should be revised, such revision having been the prime object of appointing the Commission.

" In the absence of this assistance, I must proceed to deal with the various questions to the best of my power.

"Three points suggest themselves as necessary to be dealt with :—

> "*a*. The supervision of brothels, for protective and sanitary reasons.

> "*b*. The medical inspection of the inmates, and the prevention of disease.

> "*c*. The provision of the necessary funds.

" One of the objections now raised to the Hong Kong system is that the houses are licensed to conduct a business which is contrary to the law of England, and consequently of the Colony. That this is a very serious objection cannot be denied, but, on the other hand, we have to face the undoubted fact that it would be practically impossible to enforce that law against the Chinese community ‡ of Hong Kong. Are we then to ignore the existence of these houses, to shut our

---

* None of which records has Lord Kimberley found it convenient to produce.

† No. 13 of 1879.

‡ We cannot enforce the Common Law of England which protects women from indecent assaults, but we can, and we ought, *on the ground of humanity,* to enforce an Ordinance which subjects them to indecent assaults!

eyes to the methods by which the Chinese too often keep up the supply of their inmates, and to leave these women to undergo practical slavery without an endeavour to ameliorate their condition? The answer has been from the first, and, in my opinion, must continue to be, that, *on the ground of humanity*, we cannot shrink from this duty, and that the performance of it requires that a much stricter and more direct control shall be kept over these houses than is required or would be possible in an English community. Unfortunately, this system of control has not been sufficiently distinguished from the system of medical treatment for disease which was introduced simultaneously; and powers which were intended * for the purpose of protecting the inmates have been disregarded† or viewed mainly, if not entirely, as having for their object the detection and punishment of the keepers of unlicensed houses.

"I am not disposed to give up the special powers of visitation originally provided under Mr. Labouchere's instructions,‡ with the view to affording protection to the women, and the co-operation of the respectable Chinese, which is now assured, and which has already been productive of good, as I am glad to learn from your despatch of the 13th of November, 1880,§ would naturally lose much of its efficacy unless the police, and I think also the Registrar General, possessed the power of entering these houses without waiting to obtain a special warrant for the purpose whenever a case requiring intervention is brought to their notice. In such cases prompt action may be essential, and delay might defeat the ends of justice.

"The disgusting state of some of these houses, as disclosed by the Colonial Surgeon's report of 1874, transmitted in your despatch of the 17th of September,‖ shows that the general health of the city may be jeopardised if they are left unvisited by any medical or sanitary authority, and are allowed to continue in this filthy

---

* By Mr. Labouchere.　　　　　　　　　† By the Government.

‡ We have shown that no powers affording protection to the women were provided under Mr. Labouchere's or any other instructions. The Ordinances exist to prove this.

§ No. 35.　　　　　　　　　　　　　　‖ No. 34 of 1880.

condition ; while Dr. Ayres' private memorandum (Appendix, p. 268) proves that this state of things had, in fact, led to its natural results, viz., an outbreak of typhoid fever, and that they are remediable by the exercise of the power of supervision which it is now proposed to take away from the Colonial Surgeon.

" It seems to me, therefore, that on both grounds ample powers should be given to the proper officers to visit and inspect all houses of this description, in order to carry out any protective measures which you may suggest, and to enforce such regulations requiring, at least, ordinary cleanliness, as the experience of your officers may indicate. I would refer you for assistance upon this and similar matters of sanitation to the Public Health Act, 1875 (38 & 39 Vict., cap. 55).

" It would be necessary that all these houses should be registered much as common lodging houses are in England, certificates of registration being issued instead of licenses, if that word* is thought objectionable. A fee on registration should be paid by the keepers, and the number of inmates should be limited in proportion to the size of the buildings.

" These measures for police and sanitary measures should apply to all brothels, whether used by Europeans or Chinese, though they would presumably be chiefly required for the houses for Chinese, if it be true, as is stated, that the instances of virtual slavery exist entirely in houses of this description, and if, as may reasonably be supposed, the European houses are free from the more revolting features† reported by the Colonial Surgeon in 1871.

" These regulations should be distinct from those relating to the medical inspection of women, and might be so printed in the

---

* Lord Kimberley will yet, we trust, be made to know that the objections entertained are to the fact, and not merely to the word " licensed." This coolly cynical suggestion to meet the case by a change of phrase will be regarded as an insult to the moral convictions of every opponent of the system of " State-Regulated Vice."

† These " revolting features" are material filth only. Moral filth is held of no account, as has been seen above.

Ordinance, or, if you prefer it might be included in a separate Ordinance.

"Any such measure, however, will be incomplete unless it includes penalties for keeping brothels without registration, and you should consider with the Attorney-General whether it is necessary to enact any special test which shall be deemed sufficient evidence of the existence of a brothel, or whether ordinary evidence can be relied upon in such cases.

"It will also be desirable to take summary powers for dealing with any house that, from its situation or the disorderly conduct of the inmates, creates a scandal or becomes a nuisance to the neighbours or the passers by ; and to this, *the cumberous proceedings by indictment at common law* * or under the Act 25 Geo. II., c. 36, s. 5, seem to be unsuited to the circumstances of Hong Kong, where such cases may properly be dealt with as police offences, and determined by the police magistrate.

"Upon the second question, viz., the medical inspection of women, looking to the practice in the past, and to the recommendation of yourself and of the three Commissioners on this head, I concur in thinking that the inmates of houses for the sole use of Chinese may be exempted from all liability to medical inspection. At the same time it seems proper to subject to a penalty the keeper of any such house in which a European is allowed to have intercourse with the women. The fact may be difficult of proof, but the knowledge that the penalty exists will have a *salutary* † effect.

"As regards houses used by Europeans and other foreigners, I think that the medical examination of the inmates, and their separation if found diseased, should still be enforced, but unaccompanied by certain of the provisions of the existing Ordinance. I should wish you to give careful consideration to the report of Dr. Sloggett, with which you have been furnished, and to consider

---

* The cumbrous proceedings at common law would require the evidence of the neighbours as to the reality of the nuisance or scandal.

† Upon whom ? the European, the "virtual slave," or the brothelkeeper ?

whether any better plan can be devised than the present practice of keeping lists of the inmates of the houses, and of holding the keepers responsible for the due observance of the regulations.

"It must rest with you and the local officials to work out the details of the Ordinance, but the penalties on women who become infected and transmit the disease should be omitted, and the power of breaking into unregistered houses or parts of houses without a warrant for the purpose of proving the house to be a brothel can scarcely be allowed to continue, but *some such* power will be *necessary*, as I have said before, to be used in case of emergency for the repression of serious offences against the liberty of the inmates.* The Imperial Acts† of 1866 and 1869, should be consulted and their provisions adopted whenever practicable. The enactments dealing with out-door prostitution may be retained, but such women should also be placed on the register, if one be established, and I cannot but think that a more vigorous administration of this part of the Ordinance would have improved the state of the harbour of which the condition as stated in the evidence reflects no credit upon the Colony.

"I commend to your attention the very just observations which Dr. Sloggett makes upon the conduct of the so-called ' protected '‡ women, and measures should be taken to prevent their houses becoming in future unregistered brothels for other women who are not under protection.

"It is manifest that the practice of allowing women who are under treatment to leave the hospital ' on pass ' is opposed to the principle of the regulations, and should be discontinued.

"I am at a loss to understand why these Ordinances, which are

---

* The liberty of the inmates is, we presume, to be, once again, the *intention* of a system which, as Govenor Hennessey has shown "intensifies" their slavery.

† No such repression of offences against the liberty of the inmates is provided for by the Acts.

‡ The " protected " women of Hong Kong are said, by the Commissioners, to be women living as the recognised mistress of one man, who undertakes to pay for the maintenance and education of the children.

similar to those which work satisfactorily at Singapore, should not have been equally effective at Hong Kong unless it be that all branches of the public service, police as well as medical, which are charged with enforcing the law have in the former Colony mutually assisted each other in the discharge of their respective duties, and this has not been the case at Hong Kong. I should hope that similar co-operation in the future will produce the like results in the Colony under your Government. It is obvious that the duties hitherto performed by the Inspectors of Brothels cannot be entrusted to the general body of police, and men should, as in England, be carefully selected for the work and strictly supervised in the discharge of their duties. They should be members of the police force, and subject to the general rules of the force, but for the exercise of their special functions they should report to and be immediately under the control of a particular officer, and you will inform me whether you recommend for this duty the Deputy Superintendent of Police or the Registrar-General. They should be paid from *the funds raised under the Ordinance*, and should receive sufficient emoluments to ensure the appointment of trustworthy and competent men, who must be looked for in this country if there is any difficulty in finding them in the Colony.*

---

* We would ask the reader to note that in the face of the strong opposition to the *principle* as well as to the operation of the Contagious Diseases Acts in this country, and of the fact that during the period of this correspondence a Committee of the House of Commons has been sitting to inquire into those Acts, Lord Kimberley has chosen to hold them out as a model to the Colony of Hong Kong, with the addition of such still more objectionable features as the licensing and registration of brothels; and that the authority on which he relies and the adviser whom he quotes is Mr. Sloggett.

It appears to us to be an unseemly disrespect of Parliament and of public opinion in this country thus to steal a march upon the opponents of all State-regulation of Vice, and to indorse the system here by compelling its adoption in a distant colony, against the evident opinion and wish of the Colonial Commission appointed to inquire into the subject, and of the Governor himself.

Having in mind these facts, together with the infrequent sittings and

" You may find it desirable to consult the Governor of the Straits
Settlements upon some of the details of the measures to be
prepared, and I shall be glad if you will communicate freely with
him upon any point in which the experience of that Colony may
appear likely to be useful.

" There remains the question of finance upon which I would
observe that whilst it is in my opinion indefensible to make a tax
on brothels a source of revenue to the Colony, it seems to me to
be sound in principle and just to the taxpayers that any amount
required to meet the cost of the necessary control and supervision
of these houses beyond the amount contributed by the Admiralty
should be levied on the brothel-keepers.

" Should the collections exceed the amount fairly chargeable
to all the several departments which have to do with this service,
including a due proportion of the Medical, the Police, and the
Registrar General's establishments, as well as the direct charges
of the Lock hospital and similar matters, the equilibrium between
revenue and expenditure may be maintained by increasing the
outlay should the efficiency of the service seem to require it ; or
by reducing the amount of the fees, chargeable for registration of
the houses.

" I have in conclusion to request you to take this whole subject
into your careful and early consideration, and to transmit to me,
with as little delay as possible, the draft of any Ordinance or

---

apparently unnecessary procrastination of the House of Commons' Committee
on the Contagious Diseases Acts, no one can be surprised that Mr. Stansfeld
has felt it to be his duty no longer to be put off, but to make his appeal
to Parliament this session in any event.

The existing Ordinances, with or without such modifications as Lord
Kimberley suggests, exceed in their patent immorality and unconstitution-
ality the English Acts ; but they furnish evidence to show how far our rulers
are prepared to go—when they dare—and the results which all such systems
inevitably develope. The shameless violation of the most sacred personal
rights of the weak, in the vain attempt to secure the *pleasures* of salubrious
debauchery for the strong, is the logical outcome of every system of State
regulated, organised and patented vice.

This correspondence has one merit in our eyes. It ought to cause, and
we believe that it will cause, the downfall of the system here.

Ordinances which you would propose to lay before the Legislative Council.

"In reply to your despatch of the 13th of November, * I asked, on the 31st of December,† for explanations in support of your statement that the Ordinances of 1857 and 1867 have tended to intensify the evils of brothel slavery, but I do not delay this despatch until receiving your reply, as I shall be able to address you further on that point, should it be necessary to add to what I have said above. "I have, &c.

"Sir J. Pope Hennessey." (Signed) "KIMBERLEY.

On the 28th of July, Lord Kimberley again wrote to Governor Hennessey, saying :—

"I have the honour to acknowledge the receipt of your despatch of the 15th of June,‡ in reply to mine of the 31st of December, 1880,§ asking for particulars as to Contagious Diseases Ordinances of 1857 and 1867 having caused an increase of brothel slavery.

"2. My despatch of the 26th instant,‖ communicating the conclusions at which I have arrived upon the Report of the Commission, was completed before the receipt of your despatch under acknowledgment, and I have allowed it to proceed, as I do not find that there is anything in this despatch to alter the opinions which I have expressed.

"3. You will observe that, under the proposed new regulations, the inmates of brothels used by Chinese only, which form the majority of the houses, will be exempted from all liability to medical inspection. This will remove entirely the objections stated in the fifth paragraph of your despatch.

"4. I can quite believe that the women in these houses are in great dread of their *keepers* ¶ and 'have no courage to seek their

---

* No. 35 of 1880. † No. 36 of 1880. ‡ No. 37 of 1881. § No. 36 of 1880.
‖ No. 38 of 1881.

¶ Reference to Governor Hennessey's despatch will show that he speaks of the "extraordinary dread" entertained by the women "of all foreigners," and gives evidence to prove that their terror is of the police in the first instance, and of their keepers who occupy a "semi-official position" through the boasted protection of the police and threaten any unruly inmates with surgical inspection. (See Appendix F.)

freedom." Unfortunately recent experience has shown that this state of things is not peculiar to Chinese brothels, but exists also in European countries ;† but I am not prepared to agree in the view that these unfortunate women will be benefited by the withdrawal of all control over the houses in which they are immured, although it would no doubt relieve the Government from a very disagreeable duty if matters were left to take their course, and it would probably be more in accordance with Chinese ideas and habits if no interference were attempted with their peculiar brothel institutions. I view with much satisfaction the steps taken by the respectable Chinese to co-operate with the Government in their efforts to deal with this evil, and with their aid and an intelligent and careful working of such regulations as I have suggested, I should hope that a sensible check may be given to the nefarious practices of the brothel-keepers.

"I have, &c.

(Signed)   "KIMBERLEY.

"Sir J. Pope Hennessey."

We have said that we believe that the correspondence printed above will lead to the downfall of the whole system of state-licensed and patented vice, not merely in the Colonies, but at home. For this it is only necessary that Englishmen should put all party-considerations aside and do their duty.

If they will remember that the organised iniquities which we have disclosed, were originated " by the desires of Her Majesty's Government," when that Government was " Liberal," and have since been pertinaciously upheld and maintained by Tory and Liberal Governments alike; that the actual Government, through their mouth-piece, Lord Kimberley, is even now forcing this monstrous violation of the Constitution upon an unwilling population in Hong Kong, and

----

* Why so, since the Ordinances are *intended* to protect them; the police protect them, and the Registrar General is Protector of the Chinese?

† Wheresoever the system of State-regulated Vice prevails.

that they still uphold it here in the teeth of public opinion and the moral sense of the people, the people will teach their rulers that in their eyes the safeguards of personal liberty secured to them by Magna Charta, the *Habeas Corpus* and the Bill of Rights, are not the "dream" which Sir R. MacDonnell declared them to be.

Our British Constituences have only to WILL that the rights won for them by their fathers shall not be filche d from them in the dark, and the remedy is in their own hands.

APPENDIX (A).

FORWARDING REPORT TO MR. STANSFELD.

Sir Michael Hicks Beach wrote to the Governor of Hong Kong on the 9th July, 1879, "I have observed in *The Shield* Newspaper, No. 371, of the 31st May last, mention is made of the Report now being considered by me as "an extremely interesting document," and it is stated that Mr. Stansfeld gave a short account of the results of the Hong Kong Commission. I presume from this fact, that the Report must have been published in the Colony. If it has not yet been published, I should wish you to ascertain if possible how copies can have been furnished to private persons in this country. If on the other hand, it has been given to the public, I would point out that it would have been better, considering the nature of the subject and of its history, not to have published this report until I had had the opportunity of considering it and arriving at some decision upon it." Sir J. P. Hennessey replied, pointing out that "the inquiry arose out of a public transaction, in which a coroner's jury had made a special finding that a practice which had been carried on, apparently with the sanction of the Government, was illegal and immoral, and the local newspapers from time to time demanded the publication of the proceedings. A question had been asked on the subject by Sir H. Johnstone in the House of Commons, and Sir Michael Hicks Beach's reply indicated no desire to keep the facts from the public." When the report was published, he (the Governor) sent copies to "the chief naval and military officers, to the judges and members of council, the local newspapers, some half dozen Members of Parliament who had served with him on the Select Committee on the subject in 1864, and a few others who were interested in the question, including Mr. Stansfeld." The fact that the Report had been published in the Colony did not appease the Home Government. The Hong Kong newspapers might easily have escaped Mr. Stansfeld's eye. When Lord Kimberley succeeded Sir Michael Hicks Beach, he wrote to the Governor of Hong Kong: "With respect to the explanation given in the fifth and following pages of your despatch respecting the premature distribution of the Report, I feel it incumbent upon me to point out to you that a Governor is not justified in communicating to *unofficial persons* in this country important documents which have not previously been transmitted to the Secretary of State. . . I trust I may rely upon your being careful to abstain from any such action in future."

APPENDIX (B).

The conclusions and recommendations of the Colonial Commissioners are as follows:—

"To sum up briefly the results of our inquiry, we are of opinion:—

" 1. That the prosecutions which have been conducted both under the ordinances of 1857 and of 1867, have been attended with serious scandals and abuses, and that the system of informers employed in the detection of illicit prostitution cannot be too emphatically condemned.

" 2. That, as regards the suppression or termination of unlicensed houses and unregistered prostitutes, such precautions have been ineffectual.

" 3. That the number of women under sanitary regulations has always been, as compared with those left unregulated, insignificant; and that there is no sufficient evidence to show that the spread of venereal disease has been checked or prevented, or its type modified by the operation of the Brothel Laws.

" 4. That licensed brothels for foreigners are in themselves sources of infection, and that the evidence before us points to these establishments, rather than to unlicensed houses as the causes of disease to soldiers and sailors.

" 5. That Government has exercised a sound discretion in not applying the medical clauses of the ordinances to houses for the sole use of Chinese, and that any attempt to do so would end in mischievous failure.

" 6. That Government supervision of houses for the sole use of Chinese has had no appreciably beneficial results; that the Ordinances did not contemplate or justify the licensing and regulation of such houses for purposes other than those connected with the suppression of venereal disease, and that such houses should never have been made a source of revenue.

" 7. That the employment of inspectors of brothels and interpreters has been a frequent source of abuse and corruption; that the work they have to perform is thoroughly demoralising, and that a wise discretion has been exercised* in not permitting the general body of police to be engaged in carrying out the Brothel Laws.

" 8. That the medical examination of their persons is odious to Chinese women, that it is completely opposed to their own ideas and feelings and exposes those who undergo it to the ridicule and contempt of their countrymen. That the system is disliked by the

---

* By Mr. May, Superintendent of Police, of whose wise discretion Mr. Sloggett and Lord Kimberley disapprove.

whole Chinese community and is open to the gravest misconception on their part.

"9. That the quasi official recognition of the houses of ill-fame implied by granting them licenses in return for fees paid is a very objectionable system in the existing brothel system and imposes on the Government responsibilities which it cannot adequately fulfil.

"Our conclusions being therefore on all points unfavourable to the existing brothel system, we should, had we been prepared to act altogether on our own convictions, have recommended its entire abolition and the repeal of the Ordinance: and that prostitution be dealt with solely as a matter of law and order. But as the high naval and military authorities, to whom we referred the papers, have, upon the same facts and figures as we have founded our opinions on, arrived at conclusions, as to the sanitary results of the Ordinance, which do not coincide with our own, and as we fully recognise the value of these conclusions, we recommend that all prosecutions against the keepers and inmates of unlicensed brothels, which we have been told, and which we believe, are bound up with the system of informers hitherto employed, should be definitely abandoned.

"We think it most probable that, without the compulsion of criminal liability, a class of women will be found, as heretofore, ready to enter as inmates of licensed brothels for foreigners, and to subject themselves to periodical medical examination and segregation in hospital in the event of their being infected, in consideration of the real or supposed advantage in the way of business their recognised position will afford them. But in any event we are distinctly of opinion that the continuance of the system of prosecution hitherto pursued is entirely out of the question.

"We recommend that the licenses to be granted in future should be strictly limited to the houses for the accommodation of foreigners, and that in the future houses for the sole use of Chinese should not be in any way subject to Government supervision. We can see no reason why out-door prostitutes, whether in town or harbour, should not be dealt with as heretofore under the Ordinance, great care and caution however being taken as to the evidence employed.

"We recommend that no prosecutions against women for infecting men with venereal disease be allowed to be instituted in future. We advise that both in the examination of their persons and in their medical treatment, the feelings and prejudices of the women should be consulted as far as possible. Sanitary regulations ought not to be converted into a means of punishment further than the absolute necessity of the case requires ; and we think that the less irksome and distasteful the rules for the sanitation of women are made, the less likely are they to be evaded.

"Finally we recommend that an Ordinance be laid before the Legislative Council embodying the amendments in the law which we have suggested."

APPENDIX (C).

ORDINANCE OF 1857.

Copy.)

"HONG KONG,

" ANNO VICESIMO VICTORIÆ REGINÆ,

" No. 12, of 1857.

" By His Excellency, Sir John Bowring, Knight, LL.D., **Governor** and Commander-in-Chief of the Colony of Hong Kong and its Dependencies, and Vice-Admiral of the same, Her Majesty's Plenipotentiary **and** Chief Superintendent of the **trade** of British subjects in China, with **the** advice of the Legislative **Council of** Hong Kong.

"An Ordinance **for** Checking the Spread of **Venereal Diseases.**

" 24th November, 1857.

" Whereas, it is expedient to make provision for checking the spread of venereal diseases within this Colony: Be it, therefore, enacted and ordained by His Excellency the Governor of Hong Kong, by and with the advice of the Legislative Council thereof, as follows:—

" 1.—In the interpretation of this Ordinance, the following words or phrases shall have the respective meanings hereby assigned to them, that is to say:—

"' Prostitute' shall mean any woman who shall live or reside in a registered or a declared brothel. 'Declared brothel' shall mean any house in which women live or reside, or which they frequent, for the purposes of prostitution, and which shall, in any judicial proceedings under this Ordinance be sworn or deposed to be such by any two witnesses, or which shall be declared to be such by the Registrar-General. 'Registered brothel' shall mean any house in which women live or are kept for the purposes of prostitution, and which shall be certified to be such in writing by the Registrar-General, and which shall be entered and numbered on a list or register of such houses, to be kept by the Registrar-General.

" 2.—From and after the passing of this Ordinance no person shall keep a brothel within the Colony of Hong Kong, unless the same be registered, nor unless the same be within one or other of the following districts or portions of districts—namely, Ha-wau, from Spring Gardens, Eastward; Sei-ing-Poon, from the Junction of Hollywood Road and Queen's Road, West, Westward, and Tai-ping-shan, except such parts of such districts or portions of districts as face the Queen's Road; and if any persons shall be convicted of keeping a brothel outside of such districts as aforesaid, or an unregistered brothel within the same, such person shall, for the first offence, be sentenced to pay a fine not exceeding one hundred current dollars, or to imprisonment, with or without hard labour, for a term not exceeding three months, and for the second offence to pay a fine not exceeding two hundred current dollars, or to imprisonment, with or without hard labour, for a term not exceeding six months, and for the third offence to pay a fine not exceeding five hundred current dollars, or to imprisonment, for a term not exceeding twelve months; provided always, that it may be lawful for the magistrate before whom such offender shall be brought, to punish such offender both by fine and imprisonment, or by one or other of such modes, according to his discretion: and nothing herein contained shall be taken to bar any person from indicting any brothel whatsoever as a nuisance.

" 3.—Upon the occasion of any person being for the third time convicted of such offence as is aforesaid, it shall be lawful for the magistrate before whom such conviction shall take place, by warrant under his hand, to remove all the inmates of the house wherein such offender shall have dwelt or resided, and to close up such house, and forbid the same to be reinhabited, unless he shall be satisfied that the same will be occupied in a proper and legal manner, and not as a brothel within the meaning of this Ordinance, *if situated outside* of the aforesaid districts, *or, either as a registered brothel, or in any other* PROPER AND LEGAL MANNER, *if within the said districts, or any of them*: and that every person reinhabiting such house, without a license or permission under the hand of the chief or assistant magistrate shall be liable to a penalty of not more than five hundred current dollars, or to imprisonment for a term not exceeding twelve months.

" 4.—The averment of two witnesses made on oath or by affirmation within the meaning of Ordinance No. 7, of 1857, that any house is occupied as a brothel, may be received as sufficient evidence of such fact ; and any person who shall appear, act, or behave himself or herself as master or mistress, or as the person having the care or management of any brothel, shall be deemed and taken to be the keeper thereof, and shall be liable to be punished as such, notwithstanding he or she shall not, in fact, be the real owner or keeper thereof.

" 5.—The Registrar-General shall keep a register of all brothels, and shall enter in such register the names of the keeper of each of such brothels, and also of the immediate landlord or lessor thereof, also of the Crown lessee or tenant of the plot of ground on which the same may be standing or built, and shall keep it corrected from time to time, according as such keeper, immediate landlord or lessor, or Crown lessee or tenant, respectively, may change, and according as any such house shall cease at any time to be occupied as a brothel ; and shall furnish the Colonial Secretary with a copy of such register, and shall inform him from time to time of such corrections as may from time to time be made in such register as aforesaid.

" 6.—Whenever any house shall be, in the opinion of the Registrar-General, a house in which women reside, or which they frequent for the purposes of prostitution, the Registrar-General shall forthwith declare such house to be a brothel, and shall give notice to the immediate landlord or lessor thereof, or if such immediate landlord or lessor cannot be found or ascertained, then to the Crown lessee of the plot of ground on which the same be built, that such house has been declared by him to be a brothel, and as such, comes within the provisions of the second and third Sections of this Ordinance : and in case such immediate landlord or Crown lessee or tenant shall dispute such declaration of the Registrar-General, then the party so disputing such declaration shall have an appeal to the chief or assistant magistrate, or to any two justices of the peace, sitting for any such magistrates, who are hereby empowered to adjudicate on such appeals, and whose decisions thereon shall be final.

" 7.—Brothels registered under the provisions of Section 5 of this Ordinance shall be liable to be visited by the Registrar-General, and by the superintendent, deputy-superintendent, and inspectors of police, and by the Colonial surgeon or other medical officer to be from time to time appointed under the provisions of this Ordinance ; and the Registrar-General and such several officers as aforesaid are hereby empowered to visit and inspect the condition of such brothels ; and the Colonial surgeon or such other medical officer as aforesaid is hereby empowered and required to visit each one of such registered brothels, and inspect and examine each one of the inmates therein at least once in every ten days.

" 8.—Every keeper, mistress, or manager of a registered brothel shall once in every week furnish the Registrar-General with a true report of the condition of health of each and every of the inmates of the same.

" 9.—In every registered brothel there shall be kept suspended, in some public place, a board containing, in the English and Chinese languages, a list of the names and ages of the inmates then resident in the house, and such list shall be altered from time to time according as any inmate may be absent therefrom, either by reason of leaving such house altogether, or of being removed therefrom either to gaol or hospital under the provisions of this Ordinance.

" 10.—Any brothel-keeper or prostitute who shall offer any obstacle to, or refuse to admit such Registrar-General, superintendent, or inspector of police, for the purpose of making such inspection as aforesaid, or shall refuse to submit to such inspection or examination by the Colonial surgeon or such other medical officer as aforesaid, or shall furnish a wilfully false report of the condition of health of the inmates, as is herein required, or shall not keep suspended such list of such inmates, and keep the same altered or corrected from time to time, as is herein required, as the case may be, shall for each offence be liable to a penalty of not more than 100 current dollars, or may be imprisoned, with or without hard labour, for any time not exceeding three months.

" 11.—Every prostitute, or inmate of a registered brothel, who shall be at any time declared by the Colonial surgeon, or such other medical officer as aforesaid, to be affected with any venereal disease, shall be by order of the Registrar-General, given under his hand, removed to such hospital as shall be built or set apart for women affected with venereal diseases, under the provisions of this Ordinance, and such prostitute shall be kept under the control of the medical officer of such hospital, and shall not leave, or attempt to leave the same, until properly discharged as cured by such medical officer : and on every occasion of discharging any such prostitute from the said hospital, as cured, the medical officer so discharging such prostitute, shall give her a certificate under his hand of having been so discharged, which certificate, should such prostitute return to a brothel, is to be produced and shown to the Registrar-General, or to the superinten- dent or inspector of police, whensoever the production of the same shall be by him or them demanded ; and any prostitute who shall during her continuance in such hospital refuse to submit to or obey the directions of the medical officer thereof, or shall leave, or attempt to leave, the same until she be properly discharged as cured, as aforesaid, shall be liable to be imprisoned, with or without hard labour, for any time not exceeding three months : and the expenses which may be incurred in and about the main- tenance and treatment of any such prostitute in such hospital *shall be a debt due to the Crown, and shall be paid by the keeper of the brothel* of which such prostitute shall have been an inmate, or from which she shall have been so removed, and the same in case of non-payment shall be sued for and recovered by the Registrar-General.

" 12.—If any prostitute labouring under a venereal disease, shall, *to the satisfaction of the chief or assistant magistrates,* be proved to have infected any person with such disease, such prostitute, on conviction thereof, *shall be punished by imprisonment, either in gaol or hospital, for a term not exceeding three months,* and the keeper of the brothel in which such prosti- tute shall be found shall in every such case be fined a penalty not exceeding two hundred current dollars.

" 13.—*Every keeper of a registered brothel shall pay to the Registrar- General, or his collector, the sum of four current dollars per mensem, which the Registrar-General is hereby empowered to demand and collect, and all such sums are to be paid by the Registrar-General into the Colonial Treasury.*

" 14.—All monies collected under or by virtue of Sections 13 and 19 are to be appropriated to the formation of a general fund for the purposes of this Ordinance, out of which a monthly sum (to be fixed by his Excellency in Council) is to be paid to the Colonial surgeon, or to such other medical officer as may be from time to time appointed for the purposes of this Ordinance, under the provisions of Section 7, as his remuneration for performing the duties required or imposed by this Ordinance ; and the said Colonial surgeon, or such other medical officer as aforesaid, is hereby empowered (with the sanction of his Excellency the Governor) to nominate or appoint a deputy or assistant, being a person properly qualified to act for him, in case he shall be at any time incapacitated or unable to perform such duties, or any portion of them.

"15.—Every keeper of a registered brothel shall be allowed, upon giving notice thereof to the superintendent of police. and obtaining his authority, *to employ a constable for the protection of, and the preservation of order in, such brothel,* such constables to be under the control of, and responsible to, and to be paid by, the superintendent of police, *and to wear a uniform to be chosen for the purpose, but to be solely employed about the protection of the brothel by the keeper of which each of them is employed;* and every keeper of a brothel so employing such special constable as aforesaid, shall pay quarterly in advance to the superintendent of police, a sum sufficient to cover the expenses which may be incurred in payment of the wages of, and providing the uniform for such constable, and such sum shall, in case of non-payment be sued for and recovered by the superintendent of police.

"16.—A hospital shall be built, or premises in the first instance hired, exclusively for the reception and treatment of women affected with venereal diseases, the cost of renting such premises to be defrayed out of the fund to be raised under Sections 13 and 19, and the remainder of the moneys which shall from time to time be collected under the said sections, over and above such sums as shall be applied in payment of the Colonial surgeon, or such other medical officer as aforesaid, and in payment of the expenses of renting and maintaining such premises as aforesaid, shall go and be applied to the formation of a fund for the purpose of building, fitting-up. and maintaining such hospital, and enlarging the same from time to time as may be required, and all fees directed to be levied and paid by Section 13, in case of non-payment, shall be sued for and recovered by the Registrar-General, who shall pay the same into the Colonial Treasury.

"17.—Every keeper of a licensed boarding house for seamen shall furnish to the harbour master, once in every week, a list of seamen then resident in his house, and shall report in such list as to the state of health of each seaman, so far as he may be able to ascertain the same; and every seaman who may be reported or may be otherwise discovered to be affected with a venereal disease, unless then under medical treatment, shall be removed by warrant, under the hand of the harbour master, to a hospital, where he shall be kept until he be, by the medical attendants thereof, discharged as cured, and shall have obtained from such medical attendants a certificate of his having been so discharged, which certificate he shall produce, and show to the harbour master, when required so to do; and the expenses which may be incurred in and about the maintenance and treatment of any such seaman in such hospital, shall be a debt due to the Crown, and shall be paid by such seaman; or in case of the keeper of the boarding house in which such seaman shall have resided before his removal to hospital not having reported, or having made a false report, as to the state of health of such seaman, then such expenses shall be paid by such boarding house keeper, in case it shall appear to, and be certified by, the Colonial surgeon or his deputy, or the medical attendants of the hospital to which such seaman may be removed, that the disease with which he may be affected is of such a nature as that the keeper of the boarding house could, with ordinary and reasonable observation, have ascertained its existence; and in all cases such expenses shall in case of non-payment be sued for and recovered by the harbour master on behalf of the hospital.

"18.—If any seaman affected with a venereal disease, and reported so to be by the keeper of the boarding house in which such seaman may be residing, shall refuse or offer any hindrance or obstruction to his removal to hospital; or, having been removed to hospital, shall attempt to leave the same before he shall be properly discharged cured; or having been discharged cured, shall refuse to produce his certificate of discharge when required by the harbour master or his deputy, authorised to demand the same ; or being affected with a venereal disease, shall neglect or refuse to inform the keeper of the boarding house in which he may be residing, then, and in every such case, such seaman so offending shall be liable to a fine not exceeding twenty-five current dollars, or to imprisonment, with or without hard labour, for any term not exceeding one month.

" 19.—The master of any merchant ship, before shipping any seaman, may require that such seaman shall be inspected by the Colonial surgeon, or other medical officer, who may be appointed for such purpose in connection with the harbour master's department, and who is hereby required to attend at stated hours in the forenoon and afternoon of each day at the harbour master's office for the purposes of such inspection ; and the Colonial surgeon, or such other medical officer, upon such inspection, is to give a certificate under his hand as to the state of health of such seaman, which certificate such seaman is to produce and show to the master of the ship in which he may be about to serve ; and for every such certificate there shall be paid the fee of fifty cents, *to be paid by the master, or agent, of the ship, in case such seaman should prove to be in sound health, and by the seaman himself, or the boarding house keeper with whom he shall have been residing, in case he shall prove to be affected with any venereal disease ;* such fee to be received by the harbour master, and in case of non-payment to be sued for and recovered by him, and paid into the Colonial Treasury for the purposes of this Ordinance.

" 20.—In all cases where punishment by imprisonment shall be inflicted under this Ordinance, such imprisonment may be either in gaol or in hospital, and may be with or without hard labour as the Court shall adjudge.

" 21.—In all cases in which fines shall be imposed under the provisions of any section of this Ordinance, and the brothel-keeper on whom such fine shall be imposed shall be unable to pay or discharge the same, then the same shall be recovered from the immediate landlord or lessor of such house ; and in case such landlord or lessor be not known or cannot be ascertained, then from the Crown lessee of the plot of ground on which such house may be erected or built, provided it be proved to the satisfaction of the magistrate that such Crown lessee was cognisant of the purposes for which such house shall have been let or occupied.

" 22.—No house in which any trade or business shall be carried on shall be registered, or be capable of becoming a registered brothel under the provisions of this Ordinance.

" 23.—No moneys which shall be raised under the provisions of this Ordinance by way of any fee shall at any time be applied or applicable to any purposes other than or different from the specific purposes for which the same are to be raised, and to which they are to be applied under the provisions of this Ordinance.

" 24.—His Excellency in Council is hereby empowered from time to time to make such regulations and bye-laws as may be deemed necessary for carrying into effect the provisions of this Ordinance, and for the regulation and control of registered brothels within the aforesaid districts.

" 25.—All cases arising under this Ordinance shall be tried and adjudicated by, and all fines and penalties herein mentioned, and all sums herein declared to be recoverable, shall be sued for and recovered before, any magistrate of police, *either singly*, or any two or more justices of the peace in the manner provided by Ordinance No. 10 of 1844, entitled, ' *An Ordinance to regulate Summary Proceedings before Justices of the Peace, and to protect Justices in the execution of their duty.'*

"JOHN BOWRING.

" Passed by the Legislative Council of Hong Kong,
" this 24th day of November, 1857,

"J. M. D'ALMADA E. CASTRO,
"*for the Clerk of Councils.*"

"No. 39.   Proclamation.
" John Bowring.

" By his Excellency Sir John Bowring, Knight, LL.D., Governor and Commander-in-Chief of the Colony of Hong Kong, and its dependencies and Vice-Admiral of the same, Her Majesty's Plenipotentiary and Chief Superintendent of the Trade of British Subjects in China.

" Whereas the commands of Her Most Gracious Majesty the Queen, conveyed through the Right Honourable the Principal Secretary of State for the Colonies, have been received, approving of and confirming the following* Ordinance, namely :—

" No. 12, of 1857, entitled—

" *An Ordinance for Checking the Spread of Venereal Disease.*

" Now, therefore, it is hereby declared, that the said Ordinance has been so approved and confirmed as aforesaid.

" By his Excellency's command,

" W. T. BRIDGES,

" Acting Colonial Secretary.

" God save the Queen."

" Given at Victoria, Hong Kong, this 26th April, 1858."

"The foregoing.

APPENDIX (D).

ORDINANCE 10 OF 1867.

The Hong Kong Commissioners say of this Ordinance: "A great deal of knowledge has been acquired during the ten years the old law had been in force of the feelings of the Chinese with respect to the personal examination of prostitutes and of the dread which the women entertained of the operation. It was clearly enough seen that these formed the chief causes of the paralysis of the old system, and it was therefore resolved that the new legislation should inaugurate a more vigorous policy of coercion.

"The key note of the new *régime* was struck by the Governor's first minute on the subject dated 20th October, 1866 (Document 20, p. 214), in which he wrote that he was ‘anxious early to introduce to the Council an amended brothel Ordinance conferring *necessarily** almost *despotic* powers on the Registrar General, modified, when necessary, by by-laws to be passed by the Governor in Council,’ and the Ordinance which eventually passed the legislature certainly fell but little short of his Excellency's intentions."

ORDINANCE No. 10 of 1867.

Contagious Diseases.

SIR RICHARD GRAVES MacDONNELL, Knight, C.B.,

Governor and Commander-in-Chief.

No. 10 of 1867.

TITLE.

An Ordinance enacted by the Governor of Hong Kong, with the Advice of the Legislative Council thereof for the better Prevention of Contagious Diseases.

[23rd July, 1867.]

PREAMBLE.

Whereas it is expedient to make further Provisions calculated to prevent the spreading of certain Contagious Diseases: Be it therefore enacted by the Governor of Hong Kong, with the Advice of the Legislative Council thereof, as follows:

PRELIMINARY.

I. *Short Title.*—This Ordinance may be cited as "The Contagious Diseases Ordinance, 1867."

---

* The italics are the Governor's own.

II. *Interpretation of Terms.*—In this Ordinance :—

"*Contagious Disease.*"—The Expression "Contagious Disease" means Venereal Disease including Gonorrhœa.

"*District.*"—The word "District" means a District of the City of Victoria as defined by "The Victoria Registration Ordinance, 1866."

"*Superintendent of Police.*"—The Expression "Superintendent of Police" means the Captain Superintendent of Police appointed under Ordinance No. 9 of 1862.

"*Householder*" and "*Agent.*"—The Words "Householder" and "Agent" mean a Householder and his accredited Agent as defined by "The Victoria Registration Ordinance, 1866."

"*Keeper of a Licensed Brothel.*"—The Expression "Keeper of a Licensed Brothel" means the Registered Keeper thereof and any Person appointed by a Keeper during his absence.

"*Keeper of an Unlicensed Brothel.*"—The Expression "Keeper of an Unlicensed Brothel" includes the Tenant of the House or part of the House, as the case may be, wherein the same shall be kept.

"*Inmate of a Licensed Brothel.*"—The Expression "Inmate of a Licensed Brothel" means any female residing in such Brothel.

III. *Suspending Clause.*—This Ordinance shall not come into operation until Her Majesty's confirmation thereof shall have been proclaimed in this Colony by the Governor.

IV. *Repeal of Ordinance No. 12 of 1857.*—Ordinance No. 12 of 1857 is hereby repealed, but such repeal shall not affect the Validity or Invalidity of anything done or suffered before the commencement of this Ordinance and shall not apply to or in respect of any Offence, act or thing committed or done or omitted before the commencement of this Ordinance and every such Offence, act or thing shall after and notwithstanding the commencement of this Ordinance have the same consequences and effect in all respects as if this Ordinance had not been passed.

REGISTRAR GENERAL.

V. *Power of Registrar General.*—For the purposes of carrying into effect the provisions of this Ordinance the Registrar General shall in the first instance have exclusive Jurisdiction to hear and determine all matters except where otherwise specially provided and shall have full power to do in addition to the other duties imposed upon him hereby whatever a Police Magistrate is by any Ordinance of this Colony authorised to do.

VI. *Power of appeal to the two Magistrates.*—It shall be lawful for any Person aggrieved or affected by any Order, Decision, or Proceeding of the Registrar General within the meaning of this Ordinance other than and except such proceedings as are authorised by so much thereof as is contained between Sections XX. and XXIV. both inclusive, to appeal therefrom to the Two Magistrates the Decision of whom when sitting together shall be final and conclusive; Provided always that no such appeal shall lie unless within Three clear Days after the determination by the Registrar General of any matter in respect of which an appeal is hereby allowed application shall have been made to him to state and sign a case setting forth the facts of the matter and the ground of his determination; and upon every such appeal the Registrar General shall transmit the Depositions or Minutes of Evidence taken by him to the Two Magistrates who may take such further Evidence as they shall think fit.

LICENSED BROTHELS.

VII. *Registrar General may grant Brothel Licenses.*—The Registrar General may grant to any Person whom he shall think fit a License to keep a Brothel in such District or other locality as the Governor in Council may from time to time appoint.

VIII. *No Licensed Brothel to be kept in a House, &c. where any Trade is carried on.*—No Licensed Brothel shall be kept in any House in which any Trade or Business is carried on nor in any House communicating by any Passage Door or otherwise with any House or Room in which any Trade or Business is carried on.

IX. *Cancellation or Suspension of License.*—The Registrar General may at any time cancel or suspend a License.

X. *A Register of Licensed Brothels to be kept.*—A Register of Licensed Brothels shall be kept in the Office of the Registrar General who shall cause to be entered therein :—

(1.) The name and address of every Keeper of a Licensed Brothel.

(2.) The address of every House whereof the whole or any part shall be occupied or used as a Licensed Brothel.

(3.) The name and address of the Householder of every such House or of the Tenant of every part of such House.

(4.) Any other particulars which the Registrar General may from time to time deem expedient to be entered in the said Register subject nevertheless to such Regulations as the Governor in Council may make.

XI. *Keeper of Licensed Brothel to exhibit and to furnish to the Registrar General a List of Inmates.*.—Every Keeper of a Licensed Brothel shall cause a List of the names and ages of the Inmates thereof in the English language and also in such other language as the Registrar General may direct to be affixed in some conspicuous place in such Brothel and shall cause the said List to be altered from time to time as occasion may require and shall furnish the Registrar General with a copy of such List and of all alterations made therein.

XII. *Penalty in case of any Person being infected in a Licensed Brothel.*—If any Person shall to the satisfaction of the Registrar General be proved to have been infected with a Contagious Disease in any Licensed Brothel the Keeper thereof shall be liable to a Fine not exceeding 200 dols. and the inmate thereof who shall have infected such Person as aforesaid shall be liable to Imprisonment for any Term not exceeding Six Months.

XIII. *Penalty in case of a Person infecting any Inmate of a Licensed Brothel.*—If any Person shall to the satisfaction of the Registrar General be proved to have infected with a Contagious Disease the Inmate of any Licensed Brothel such person shall be liable to a fine not exceeding 200 dols. or to Imprisonment for any term not exceeding Six Months.

XIV. *Penalty for allowing any Child under the age of 15 to be in a Licensed Brothel.*—If any Child being in the opinion of the Registrar General above Eight and under Fifteen Years of age be found in any Licensed Brothel the Keeper thereof shall be liable to a Fine not exceeding 100 dols. or to Imprisonment with or without Hard Labour for any Term not exceeding One Month for the first Offence, Three Months for the second Offence, and Six Months for the third or any subsequent Offence.

XV. *Inspection of Licensed Brothels.*—Every Licensed Brothel shall be liable to be inspected at all times by the Registrar General, the Inspector of Hospitals, the Visiting Surgeons, the Superintendent of Police, and any Person who may be deputed by them respectively for the purpose of such inspection, and every Keeper of such Brothel and every other Person whomsoever who shall offer any obstacle or resistance to such inspection shall be liable to Imprisonment with or without Hard Labour for any Term not exceeding Six Months or to a Fine not exceeding 200 dols.

XVI. *Keeper of Licensed Brothel to reside therein and appoint Substitute during absence.*—Every Keeper of a Licensed Brothel shall reside therein and shall not absent himself from the Colony without giving notice to the Registrar General and appointing some Person to act as Keeper thereof during his absence, and in every case where the Keeper of a Licensed Brothel shall fail to comply with the requirements of this Section, the License granted in respect of such Brothel shall become *ipso facto* void.

XVII. *Recovery of Fines on Keeper of Registered Brothel.*—The Provisions of Sections XVII., XVIII., and XIX. of "The Victoria Registration Ordinance. 1866," shall apply to the recovery of any Fine imposed upon the Keeper of a Licensed Brothel.

XVIII. *Fees payable for a Brothel License.*—Every Keeper of a Licensed Brothel shall pay to the Registrar General the sum of 4 dols. a month during the continuance of such License or such other sum as may from time to time be fixed by the Governor in Council.

UNLICENSED BROTHELS.

XIX. *No Unlicensed Brothels to be kept.*—From and after the passing of this Ordinance no Person shall keep a Brothel unless the same shall have been licensed and registered as hereinbefore in that behalf provided.

XX. *Power to enter or break into Houses suspected of being Unlicensed Brothels.*—Whenever the Registrar General or the Superintendent of Police shall have reason to suspect that any House or portion of a House is used as an Unlicensed Brothel, it shall be lawful for them or either of them and for any Constables or other Persons deputed by them or either of them for the purpose at any time without warrant to enter, and if necessary to break into such House or portion of a House and to take into custody any Person who shall appear, act, or behave himself as the Person having the care or management of such House or Portion of a House so suspected as aforesaid and such Person shall be brought forthwith before the Registrar General who may as he shall think fit order such Person to be discharged from custody or may deal with him or her under the Provisions of Section XXI. of Ordinance No. 8 of 1858.

XXI. *Investigation by Registrar General as to suspected Brothel.*—It shall be lawful for the Registrar General whenever he shall have reason to suspect that a House or a portion of a House is used as an Unlicensed Brothel to institute an Investigation with reference thereto and for such purpose or for the purpose of any appeal under Section XXIV. to summon in writing before him the Householder or his Agent and any Tenant or occupier of any portion of such House and all other Persons capable of giving Evidence in such matter and to examine them upon oath touching the subject of such Investigation and any person who shall neglect or refuse to appear before the Registrar General at the time and place specified in such summons or to answer all questions which may be put to him in the course of such examination shall be liable to a Fine not exceeding 500 dols. or to be Imprisoned with or without Hard Labour for any Term not exceeding Six Months and in the event of his giving false testimony in the course of such examination he shall be liable to be tried and punished for Perjury and for that purpose every such Investigation shall be deemed a Judicial Proceeding.

XXII. *Notice of such Investigation.*—The Registrar General shall give notice of such Investigation by advertisement in the *Gazette* and also to the parties interested in the Land whereon such House shall be situate so far as they can be ascertained by reference to the Records of the Land Office but the want of such notice shall not invalidate any Proceedings.

XXIII. *Declaration by Registrar General that a House or Part of a House is an Unlicensed Brothel.*—The Registrar General shall take notes of the Evidence given during such Investigation and if he shall be of opinion that such House or part of a House as aforesaid is an Unlicensed Brothel he shall declare the same to be such under his hand and seal of office and a Notification of such Declaration shall be inserted in the *Gazette* as soon as practicable after the making thereof. A copy of the *Gazette* containing such Notification shall be conclusive evidence of such Declaration, and of the fact that such House or part of a House is an Unlicensed Brothel subject nevertheless to appeal as hereinafter provided.

XXIV. *Appeal from such Declaration to Judge of Court of Summary Jurisdiction.*—Any person aggrieved or affected by any such Declaration may within Ten Days from the date of the Notification thereof in the *Gazette*, or at any time by leave of the Judge of the Court of Summary Jurisdiction appeal from the Decision of the Registrar General to the said Judge and the Registrar General shall, upon notice of such appeal forthwith transmit to the said Judge the notes of the Evidence taken by him during such Investigation and upon which such Declaration shall have been made, and for the purpose of such appeal shall take and transmit in manner aforesaid such further evidence as the said Judge shall direct and the said Minutes and further evidence if any shall be laid before the said Judge who may confirm the said Declaration or may order in writing the same to be cancelled.

XXV. *Who shall be deemed Keeper of an Unlicensed Brothel.* — Any Person who shall appear, act, or behave himself as the Person having the Care or Management of any Unlicensed Brothel shall be deemed and taken to be the Keeper thereof and shall be liable to be punished as such notwithstanding he may not in fact be the Keeper thereof.

XXVI. *Penalty on Women residing in or frequenting Unlicensed Brothels for purposes of Prostitution.*—Every Woman who shall reside in, frequent, or be found in an Unlicensed Brothel for the purposes of Prostitution shall upon proof thereof to the satisfaction of the Registrar General be liable to a Fine not exceeding 50 dols. or to Imprisonment for any Term not exceeding Two Months.

XXVII. *Penalty for keeping Unlicensed Brothel.*—Every Keeper of an Unlicensed Brothel shall be liable for the first Offence to a Fine not exceeding 100 dols. or to imprisonment with or without Hard Labour for a Term not exceeding Three Months, for the second Offence to a Fine not exceeding 200 dols. or to Imprisonment with or without Hard Labour for a Term not exceeding Six Months, and for a third and any subsequent Offence to a Fine not exceeding 500 dols. or to Imprisonment with or without Hard Labour for a Term not exceeding Twelve Months : Provided always that it shall be lawful for the Registrar General to punish such Offender both by Fine an Imprisonment if he shall think fit.

XXVIII. *Premises twice declared to be used as an Unlicensed Brothel may be closed up.*—Whenever any House or part of a House shall have been twice declared by the Registrar General to be an Unlicensed Brothel it shall be lawful for him by Warrant under his hand to remove all the Inmates of such House or part of a House as the case may be and to close up the same and such House or part of a House shall not be re-inhabited unless the Registrar General shall be satisfied that the same will be occupied in a proper and legal manner and not as an Unlicensed Brothel, or unless the Governor shall otherwise direct and permit ; and every Person knowingly re-inhabiting any House or part of a House so closed up as aforesaid without the Permission of the Governor or of the Registrar General shall be liable to a Fine not exceeding 200 dols. or to Imprisonment with or without Hard Labour for any Term not exceeding Six Months.

XXIX. *Saving of other Remedies.*—Nothing herein contained shall as regards Unlicensed Brothels affect any other remedies applicable by the Laws in force in the Colony for the time being for the Suppression thereof.

OUTDOOR PROSTITUTION.

XXX. *Woman found in Street, &c., for purposes of Prostitution liable to Fine and Imprisonment*—Every Woman who shall be found in any Street, Road, Matshed, or other Place within One Mile of any District for the purposes of Prostitution shall be liable to a Penalty not exceeding 25 dols. or to be imprisoned for any Term not exceeding Three Months with or without Hard Labour.

XXXI. *Woman found on board any Junk, &c., for purposes of Prostitution liable to Fine and Imprisonment.*—Every Woman who shall be found on board of any Junk, Boat, Sampan, or Craft of any kind or description within Colonial Waters, for the purposes of Prostitution shall be liable to a Penalty not exceeding 25 dols., or to be imprisoned for any Term not exceeding Three Months with or without Hard Labour.

XXXII. *Person in charge of Junk, &c. in which Woman found for purposes of Prostitution liable to Fine and Imprisonment, and Junk, &c., to forfeiture.*—Every Person apparently in charge of any Junk, Boat, Sampan, or Craft when any Woman shall be found therein for the purposes of Prostitution shall be liable to the same penalties as in the last preceeding Section mentioned and in addition thereto such Junk, Boat, Sampan or Craft, may on proof of any Woman having been found therein for the purposes aforesaid be forfeited to the Crown.

XXXIII. *Constable authorized to arrest without Warrant Persons found offending and to seize Junk, &c.*—It shall be lawful for any Constable belonging to the Police Force to take into Custody without Warrant any Person in any manner offending against the Three last preceding Sections and to seize, detain and take possession of any Junk, Boat, Sampan, or Craft in which any Woman shall be found for the purpose aforesaid.

INSPECTOR OF HOSPITALS AND SURGEONS.

XXXIV. *Appointment of Inspector of Hospitals and Visiting Surgeons.*—An Inspector of Hospitals and Visiting Surgeons shall be appointed whose respective duties shall from time to time be defined by the Governor. Until the Governor shall otherwise direct and during any vacancy the Colonial Surgeon shall be Inspector of Hospitals,

HOSPITALS.

XXXV. *Power to Governor to provide Hospitals.*—The Governor may from time to time provide any Buildings or parts of Buildings as Hospitals for the purposes of this Ordinance and the fact of such Buildings or parts of Buildings being so provided shall be notified in the *Gazette*. A copy of the *Gazette* containing any such Notification shall be conclusive evidence thereof.

XXXVI. *Superintendent of Hospital.* — A Superintendent shall be appointed for each Hospital who shall have the control and management thereof, subject nevertheless to the directions of the Inspector of Hospitals and to any Regulations made and approved under this Ordinance in respect thereof.

XXXVII. *Power to make Regulations for Hospitals.*—The Inspector of Hospitals shall make Regulations for the management and government of every Hospital as far as regards Women authorized by this Ordinance to be detained therein for Medical Treatment or being therein under Medical Treatment for a Contagious Disease such Regulations not being inconsistent with the Provisions of this Ordinance and may from time to time alter any such Regulations ; but all such Regulations and all Alterations thereof shall be subject to the approval in writing of the Governor in Council.

XXXVIII. *Evidence of Regulations.*—A printed copy of Regulations purporting to be Regulations of a Hospital so approved such copy being signed by the Inspector of Hospitals shall be evidence of the Regulations of the Hospital and of the due making and approval thereof for the purposes of this Ordinance.

XXXIX. *Care and treatment of Women detained in Hospital.*—Every Woman detained in a Hospital shall during the period of such detention be carefully provided for and furnished free of expense to her with lodging, clothing and food.

XL. *Expenses of treatment of Women in Hospitals.*—The expenses which may be incurred in or about the treatment of any Prostitute detained in a Hospital as specified in the last preceding Section shall be a Debt due to the Crown and payable by the Keeper of the Brothel or by the Keeper or Person apparently in charge of the House wherein such Person may have been residing. The same in case of non-payment may be sued for and recovered from such Keeper or Person by the Registrar General, or other duly authorized Officer, subject nevertheless to the Provisions in the next Section contained.

XLI. *Amount to be certified by Visiting Surgeon.*—No Keeper of a Licensed Brothel shall be liable to such payment unless the amount thereof shall have been certified under the hand of the Visiting Surgeon to be in accordance with a scale of charges to be from time to time fixed by the Inspector of Hospitals with the approval of the Governor and such Certificate shall be evidence of the due making and approval of such scale of charges for the purposes of this Ordinance, and of all other facts therein certified.

XLII. *In case of non-payment License to become void and amount recoverable from Householder.*—In case the Keeper of a Licensed Brothel shall refuse or neglect to pay to the Registrar General the amount due to the Crown and payable by him in respect of such expenses as aforesaid within Three Days after the service upon him of a notice in that behalf or within such further period as the Registrar General may allow the License granted to such Keeper in respect of such Brothel shall from the expiration of the said Three Days or such further period as aforesaid be suspended until such payment shall have been made or recovered, and the Provisions of Section XVII. as to the Recovery of Fines shall be applicable to the Recovery of the said amount.

MEDICAL EXAMINATION.

XLIII. *Inmates of Licensed Brothels at all times liable to Medical Examination.*—Every Inmate of a Licensed Brothel shall be liable at all times to Medical Examination by a Visiting Surgeon in such Brothel or at such Hospital as he shall direct.

XLIV. *On Information the Registrar General may issue Notice to Common Prostitute.*—Where an Information on Oath is laid before the Registrar General by the Superintendent or an Inspector of Police charging to the Effect that the Informant has good cause to believe that a Woman therein named is a common Prostitute, and is resident within a District of Victoria or if not being so resident has within Fourteen Days before the laying of the Information been within a District of Victoria or within the Harbour thereof for the purpose of Prostitution the Registrar General may if he thinks fit issue a notice thereof addressed to such Woman which notice the Superintendent or Inspector of Police shall cause to be served on her.

XLV. *Power to Registrar General to order periodical Medical Examination.*—In either of the following cases namely:—

    1st. If the Woman on whom such a notice is served appears herself or by some Person on her behalf at the time and place appointed in the notice or at some other time and place appointed by adjournment.

2nd. If she does not appear and it is shown to the satisfaction of the Registrar General that the notice was served on her a reasonable time before the time appointed for her appearance or that reasonable notice of such adjournment was given to her (as the case may be) ;

the Registrar General on Oath being made before him substantiating the matter of the Information to his satisfaction may if he think fit order that the Woman be subject to a periodical Medical Examination by a Visiting Surgeon for any period not exceeding One Year for the purpose of ascertaining at the time of each such examination whether she is affected with a Contagious Disease and thereupon she shall be subject to such a periodical Medical Examination and the Order shall be a sufficient warrant for a Visiting Surgeon to conduct such Examination accordingly.

The Order shall specify the time and place at which the Woman shall attend for the first examination.

The Superintendent of Police shall cause a copy of the Order to be served on the Woman.

XLVI. *Power to make Regulations as to Medical Examinations.* — The Governor in Council may from time to time make Regulations respecting the times and places of Medical Examinations under this Ordinance, and generally respecting the arrangements for the conduct of those Examinations ; and a copy of all such Regulations from time to time in force shall be sent to the Registrar General. the Inspector of Hospitals, the Visiting Surgeons, and the Superintendent of Police.

XLVII. *Visiting Surgeon to prescribe times, &c.* —The Visiting Surgeon having regard to the Regulations aforesaid and to the circumstances of each case shall at the first examination of each Woman examined by him and afterwards from time to time as occasion requires prescribe the times and places at which she is required to attend again for Examination and he shall from time to time give or cause to be given to each such Woman notice of the times and places so prescribed.

XLVIII. *Voluntary Submission by Woman.* —Any Woman may voluntarily by a submission in writing signed by her in the presence of and attested by the Registrar General subject herself to periodical Medical Examination under this Ordinance for any period not exceeding One Year.

DETENTION IN HOSPITAL.

XLIX. *Certificate of Visiting Surgeon.* —If on any Medical Examination under this Ordinance the Woman examined is found to be affected with a Contagious Disease she shall thereupon be liable to be detained in a Hospital subject and according to the Provisons of this Ordinance and a Visiting Surgeon shall sign a Certificate to the Effect that she is affected with a Contagious Disease naming the Hospital in which she is to be placed. Such Certificate shall be sent to the Registrar General and the Woman shall be detained in such Hospital until discharged therefrom as in the next succeeding Section mentioned or under the Provisions of Section LI. of this Ordinance.

L. *Detention in Hospital.* —Where a Woman certified by a Visiting Surgeon to be affected with a Contagious Disease is placed as aforesaid in a Hospital for Medical Treatment she shall be detained there for the purpose by a Visiting Surgeon until dischaged by him by writing under his hand.

The Certificate of a Visiting Surgeon shall be sufficient authority for such Detention.

LI. *Power to transfer to another Certified Hospital.* —The Inspector of Hospitals may if in any case it seems to him expedient by Order in writing signed by him direct the Transfer of any Woman detained in a Hospital for Medical Treatment from that Hospital to another named in the Order.

Every such Order shall be sent to the Registrar General and shall also be sufficient authority for the Superintendent of Police or any Person acting under his Order to transfer the Woman to whom it relates from the one Hospital to the other and to place her there for Medical Treatment and she shall be detained there for that purpose by the Visiting Surgeon until discharged by him by writing under his hand.

The Order of the Inspector of Hospitals shall be sufficient authority for such Detention.

LII. *Limitation of Detention.*—Provided always that no Woman shall be detained under any one Certificate for a longer time than Three Months unless the Visiting Surgeon certify that her further Detention for Medical Treatment is requisite in which case she may be further detained in the Hospital in which she is at the expiration of the said Period of Three Months by the Visiting Surgeon until discharged by him by writing under his hand.

LIII. *Power to apply for discharge*—If any Woman detained in any Hospital considers herself entitled to be discharged therefrom and the Visiting Surgeon refuses to discharge her such Woman shall on her request be conveyed before the Registrar General and he shall if satisfied upon Medical Examination that she is free from a Contagious Disease discharge her from such Hospital and such Order of Discharge shall have the same Effect as the Discharge of the Visiting Surgeon.

REFUSAL TO BE EXAMINED, &c.

LIV. *Penalty for refusal to be examined, &c.*—In the following cases, namely :—

(1.) If any Woman who is the Inmate of a Licensed Brothel or who is subjected by Order of the Registrar General under this Ordinance to periodical Medical Examination at any time temporarily absents herself in order to avoid submitting herself to such Examination on any occasion on which she ought so to submit herself or refuses or wilfully neglects to submit herself to such Examination on any such occasion ;

(2.) If any Woman authorised by this Ordinance to be detained in a Hospital for Medical Treatment quits the Hospital without being discharged therefrom by the Visiting Surgeon by writing under his hand (the Proof whereof shall lie on the accused) ;

(3.) If any Woman authorised by this Ordinance to be detained in a Hospital for Medical Treatment or any Woman being in a Hospital under Medical Treatment for a Contagious Disease refuses or wilfully neglects while in the Hospital to conform to the Regulations thereof made and approved under this Ordinance ;

then and in every such case such Woman shall be guilty of an Offence against this Ordinance and on a summary conviction shall be liable to Imprisonment with or without Hard Labour in the case of a first Offence for any term not exceeding One Month, and in a case of a second or any subsequent Offence for any term not exceeding Three Months, and in case of the Offence of quitting the Hospital without being discharged as aforesaid, the Woman may be taken into Custody without Warrant by any Constable.

LV. *Effect of Order of Imprisonment for absence, &c., from Examination.*—If any Woman is convicted of and Imprisoned for the Offence of absenting herself or of refusing or neglecting to submit herself to Examination as aforesaid, the Order subjecting her to periodical Medical Examination shall be in force after and notwithstanding her Imprisonment unless a Visiting Surgeon appointed under this Ordinance at the time of her discharge from Imprisonment certifies in writing to the Effect that she is then free from a Contagious Disease (the Proof of which Certificate shall lie on her) and in that case the Order subjecting her to periodical Medical Examination shall on her Discharge from Imprisonment cease to operate.

LVI. *Effect of Order of Imprisonment for quitting Hospital, &c.*—If any Woman is convicted of and Imprisoned for the Offence of quitting a Hospital without being discharged or of refusing or neglecting while in a Hospital to conform to the Regulations thereof as aforesaid, the Certificate of the Visiting Surgeon under which she was detained in the Hospital shall continue in force and on the expiration of her term of Imprisonment she shall be sent back from the Prison to that Hospital and shall (notwithstanding anything in this Ordinance) be detained there under that Certificate as if it were given on the day of the expiration of her term of Imprisonment unless a Visiting Surgeon appointed under this Ordinance at the time of her Discharge from Imprisonment certifies in writing to the Effect that she is then free from a Contagious Disease (the Proof of which Certificate shall lie on her) and in that case the Certificate under which she was detained and the Order subjecting her to periodical Medical Examination shall on her Discharge from Imprisonment cease to operate.

LVII. *Penalty on Woman dischaged uncured conducting herself as a Prostitute.*—If on any Woman leaving a Hospital a Notice is given to her by the Visiting Surgeon to the Effect that she is still affected with a Contagious Disease and she is afterwards in any place for the purpose of Prostitution without having previously received from one of the Visiting Surgeons appointed under this Ordinance a Certificate in writing (Proof of which Certificate shall lie on her) to the Effect that she is then free from a Contagious Disease she shall be guilty of an Offence against this Ordinance and on summary conviction before the Registrar General shall be liable to be Imprisoned with or without Hard Labour in the case of a first Offence for any term not exceeding One Month, and in the case of a second or any subsequent Offence for any term not exceeding Three Months.

DURATION OF ORDER.

LVIII. *Order to operate whenever from time to time the Woman is within the Colony but not for more than One Year.*—Every Order under this Ordinance subjecting a Woman to periodical Medical Examination shall be in operation and enforceable in manner in this Ordinance provided so long as and whenever from time to time the Woman to whom it relates is within the Colony but not in any case for a longer Period than One Year and where the Visiting Surgeon on the Discharge by him of any Woman from the Hospital certifies that she is free from Contagious Disease (Proof of which Certificate shall lie on her) the Order subjecting her to periodical Medical Examination shall thereupon cease to operate.

RELIEF FROM EXAMINATION.

LIX. *Application for Relief from Examination.*—If any Woman subjected to a periodical Medical Examination under this Ordinance (either on her own submission or under the Order of the Registrar General) desiring to be relieved therefrom and not being under detention in a Hospital makes application in writing in that behalf to the Registrar General he shall appoint by notice in writing a time and place for the hearing of the application and shall cause the notice to be delivered to the applicant and a copy of the application and of the notice to be delivered to the Superintendent of Police.

LX. *Order for Relief from Examination on Discontinuance of Prostitution.*—If on the hearing of the application it is shown to the satisfaction of the Registrar General that the applicant has ceased to be a common Prostitute or if the applicant with the approval of the Registrar General enters into a

Recognizance with or without Sureties as to the Registrar General seems meet for her good Behaviour during Three Months thereafter the Registrar General shall order that she be relieved from periodical Medical Examination.

LXI. *Forfeiture of Recognizance by Return to Prostitution.*—Every such Recognizance shall be deemed to be forfeited if at any time during the term for which it is entered into the Woman to whom it relates is in any public Thoroughfare, Street or Place or in any Junk, Boat, Sampan or Craft for the purpose of Prostitution or otherwise conducts herself as a common Prostitute.

PENALTIES FOR HARBOURING.

LXII. *Penalty for permitting Diseased Prostitute to resort to any House for Prostitution.*—If any Person being the Occupier of any House, Room or Place, or being a Manager or Assistant in the management thereof having reasonable cause to believe any Woman to be a common Prostitute and to be affected with a Contagious Disease induces or suffers her to resort to or be in that House, Room or Place for the purpose of Prostitution he shall be guilty of an Offence against this Ordinance and on summary Conviction thereof before the Registrar General shall be liable to a penalty not exceeding 100 dols. or at the discretion of the Registrar General to be Imprisoned for any Term not exceeding Six Months with or without Hard Labour.

SEAMEN AND BOARDING HOUSES FOR SEAMEN.

LXIII. *Keepers of Licensed Boarding Houses for Seamen to furnish Harbour Master with weekly Lists of the Seamen resident in their Houses, and report their state of Health. Diseased Seamen to be removed to a Hospital.*—Every Keeper of a Licensed Boarding House for Seamen shall furnish to the Harbour Master, once in every Week, a List of Seamen then resident in his House, and shall report in such List as to the state of Health of each Seamen so far as he may be able to ascertain the same; and every Seaman who may be reported or may be otherwise discovered to be affected with a Contagious Disease, shall be removed by Warrant under the Hand of the Harbour Master to a Hospital, where he shall be kept until he be, by the Visiting Surgeon thereof, discharged as cured, and shall have obtained from such Visiting Surgeon a Certificate of his having been so discharged which Certificate he shall produce and show to the Harbour Master when required so to do; and the Expenses which may be incurred in and about the Maintenance and Treatment of any such Seaman in such Hospital, shall be a Debt due to the Crown, and shall be paid by such Seaman; or, in case of the Keeper of the Boarding House in which such Seaman shall have resided before his removal to Hospital not having reported, or having made a false Report as to the state of Health of such Seaman, then such Expenses shall be paid by such Boarding House Keeper, in case it shall appear to, and be certified by, the Visiting Surgeon of the Hospital to which such Seaman may be removed, that the Disease with which he may be affected is of such a Nature as that the Keeper of the Boarding House could, with ordinary and reasonable Observation, have ascertained its Existence; and in all Cases such Expenses shall in case of non-payment be sued for and recovered by the Harbour Master on behalf the Hospital.

LXIV. *Penalty for offering any Obstruction to removal to Hospital.*—If any Seaman affected with a Contagious Disease, and reported so to be by the Keeper of the Boarding House in which such Seaman may be residing, shall refuse or offer any Hindrance or Obstruction to his Removal to a Hospital: or having been removed to a Hospital, shall attempt to leave the same before he shall be properly discharged cured; or having been discharged cured, shall refuse to produce his Certificate of Discharge when required by the Harbour Master authorized to demand the same; or being affected with a Contagious Disease, shall neglect or refuse to inform the Keeper of the Boarding House in which he may be residing,—then, and in every such case, such Seaman so offending shall be liable to be brought before the Harbour Master and subjected to a Fine not exceeding Twenty-five Dollars, or to Imprisonment with or without Hard Labor, for any Term not exceeding One Month.

LXV. *Masters of Ships before shipping Seamen may require them to undergo Medical inspection.*—The Master of any Merchant Ship, before shipping any Seaman, may require that such Seaman shall be inspected by the Colonial Surgeon by notice in writing to that effect addressed to the Harbour Master or a Visiting Surgeon appointed in pursuance of this Ordinance and the Colonial Surgeon or such Visiting Surgeon upon such Inspection is to give a Certificate under his Hand as to the State of Health of such Seaman which Certificate such seaman is to produce and show to the Master of the Ship in which he may be about to serve; and for every such Certificate there shall be paid the Fee of Fifty Cents, to be paid by the Master or Agent of the Ship in case such Seaman should prove to be in sound Health, and by the Seaman himself or the Boarding House Keeper with whom he shall be residing in case he shall prove to be affected with any Contagious Disease; such Fee to be received by the Harbour Master, and in case of non-payment to be sued for and recovered by him, and paid into the Colonial Treasury for the Purposes of this Ordinance.

EXPENSES OF EXECUTION OF ORDINANCE.

LXVI. *Fines and Fees levied and collected to form a General Fund.*—All Fines imposed and levied for Offences against this Ordinance and all Fees and payments collected under the Provisions thereof shall be appropriated to the formation of a General Fund for the purposes of this Ordinance.

APPOINTMENT OF OFFICERS, BYE-LAWS, REGULATIONS, &c.

LXVII. *Power to Governor to appoint all Officers.*—The Governor shall from time to time appoint all Officers employed in carrying out the Provisions of this Ordinance and the Duties and Salaries of all such Officers shall be regulated from time to time by the Governor in Council.

LXVIII. *Power to Governor in Council to make Bye-Laws.*—The Governor in Council may from time to time make such Regulations and Bye-Laws as may be deemed necessary for carrying into Effect the Provisions of this Ordinance and for the control of Licensed Brothels.

LXIX. *Bye-Laws to take effect Seven Days after Publication in Gazette.* —No such Regulation or Bye-Laws shall take effect until Seven Days after the Publication thereof in the *Gazette* and a copy of the *Gazette* containing such Publication shall be conclusive Evidence of such Regulations or Bye-Laws.

PROCEDURE.

LXX. *Place of Proceeding before Registrar General to be fixed by Governor and shall not be in open Court unless by desire of party affected.*—The Place in which the Registrar General shall sit in discharge of his duties shall be such place as may from time to time, be appointed for that purpose by the Governor, and the Place in which any Proceeding under this Ordinance before the Registrar General or on appeal shall take place, shall not, unless the Person accused or affected by such Proceedings so desires, be deemed an open Court and unless such Person otherwise desires the Registrar General, the Magistrates, or the Judge of the Court of Summary Jurisdiction as the case may be, may order that no Person have access to or be or remain in that Place without permission.

LXXI. *Every offence against this Ordinance a Misdemeanour.* Every

Person violating the Provisions of this Ordinance or of any Regulation or Bye-Laws made in pursuance thereof shall be guilty of a Misdemeanour and except where otherwise provided by this Ordinance or by any Regulations or Bye-Laws made as aforesaid shall be liable on Summary Conviction before the Registrar General to a Fine not exceeding 200 dollars or to Imprisonment with or without Hard Labour for any Term not exceeding Six Months.

LXXII. *Forms in Schedule may be used.*—The forms of Certificates, Orders, and other Instruments given in the Schedule to this Ordinance or Forms to the like effect with such variations and additions as circumstances require may be used for the purposes therein indicated and according to the directions therein contained and Instruments in those forms shall (as regards the Form thereof) be valid and sufficient.

LXXIII. *Presumption in favour of authenticity of Signatures, &c.*—In any Proceeding under this Ordinance every Notice, Order, Certificate, Copy of Regulations, or other Instrument shall be presumed to have been duly signed by the Person and in the Character by whom and in which it purports to be signed until the contrary is shown.

LXXIV. *Mode of Service.*—Every Notice, Order or other Instrument by this Ordinance required to be served on a Woman shall be served by Delivery thereof to some Person for her at her usual Place of abode or by Delivery thereof to her personally.

LXXV. *Judge, &c. to frame Rules for regulating Appeals.*—For the purpose of regulating Appeals under this Ordinance, the Judge of the Court of Summary Jurisdiction and the Magistrates respectively shall frame Rules, Orders and Forms, and may from time to time amend such Rules, Orders or Forms, and such Rules, Orders and Forms or amended Rules, Orders or Forms certified under the hand of the said Judge or under the hands of the said Magistrates as the case may be shall be submitted to the Legislative Council who may allow, disallow or alter the same.

LXXVI. *Limitation of Actions, &c.*—Any Action, Plaint or Prosecution against any Person for anything done in pursuance or execution or intended execution of this Ordinance or of any Regulations or Bye-Laws made in pursuance thereof shall be commenced within Three Months after the thing done and not otherwise.

Notice in writing of every such Action or Plaint and of the cause thereof shall be given to the intended Defendant One Month at least before the Commencement of the Action or Plaint.

In any such Action or Plaint the Defendant may plead generally or set up by way of Special Defence that the Act complained of was done in pursuance or execution or intended execution of this Ordinance or of any such Regulation or Bye-Law as aforesaid and give this Ordinance and such Regulation or Bye-Law and the special matter in Evidence at any trial to be had thereupon.

The Plaintiff shall not recover if Tender of sufficient amends is made before Action or Plaint brought or if after Action or Plaint brought a sufficient Sum of Money is paid into Court by or on behalf of the Defendant.

If a Verdict passes or Decree is given for the Defendant or the Plaintiff becomes nonsuit or discontinues the action after Issue joined or if on Demurrer or otherwise Judgment is given against the Plaintiff, the Defendant shall recover his full Costs and shall have the like remedy for the same as any Defendant has by Law for Costs in other Cases.

Though a Verdict or Decree is given for the Plaintiff he shall not have costs against the Defendant unless the Judge before whom the Trial is had certifies his approbation of the action or Plaint.

SCHEDULES.

(A.)

(Gazette Notice of Appointments.)

"THE CONTAGIOUS DISEASES ORDINANCE, 1867."

His Excellency the Governor has been pleased to appoint [   ]
to be [   ] under the above mentioned Ordinance.

By Order,

——————.
Colonial Secretary.

Colonial Secretary's Office, Hongkong. [date].

(B.)

(Notification of Hospital.)

"THE CONTAGIOUS DISEASES ORDINANCE, 1867."

In pursuance of the above mentioned Ordinance it is hereby notified that His Excellency the Governor has provided the following Building (or part of a Building) namely [*Here describe the same generally*] as a Hospital for the purposes of this Ordinance.

By Order,

——————,
Colonial Secretary.

Colonial Secretary's Office. Hong Kong, [date].

(C.)

(Information.)

"THE CONTAGIOUS DISEASES ORDINANCE, 1867."

Hong-Kong) The Information of [   ] Superintendent
to wit.   ) [or Inspector] of Police taken this   Day of
       18   before the undersigned who says he has good cause to believe that [   ] is a Common Prostitute and (is resident within a District of Victoria that is to say [*state address*]) (or "was within 14 Days before the laying of this Information within a District of Victoria or within the Harbour thereof for the purpose of Prostitution.")

Taken and sworn before me the Day and Year first above mentioned.

(Signed.)   ——————,
Registrar General.

(D.)

(Notice for Attendance of Women.)

"THE CONTAGIOUS DISEASES ORDINANCE, 1867."

To *A. B.* of

Take notice that an Information a Copy whereof is subjoined hereto has been laid before me and that in accordance with the provisions of the above mentioned Ordinance the Truth of the Statements therein contained will be inquired into before me at
on the   Day of   18   at   o'clock in the   noon.

You are therefore to appear **before me at that** Place and Time **and to**
answer to what is stated in the said Information.

You may appear **yourself or by any person on** your Behalf.

If you do not **appear you may be ordered** without further **Notice to be**
subject to a periodical Medical Examination by the Visiting Surgeon under
the said Ordinance.

If you prefer it, you may by a Submission in writing signed by you in my
presence and attested by me subject yourself to such a periodical Examination.

If you do so before the Time above appointed for your appearance it will
not be necessary for you to appear before me.

Dated this   Day of   18   .

                                        (Signed,) ————————,
                                                      Registrar General.

[*Subjoin Copy of Information.*]

————

(E.)

(Order subjecting Women to Examination.)

"THE CONTAGIOUS DISEASES ORDINANCE. 1867."

Hong Kong ⎫ Be it remembered, that on the   Day of
to wit.   ⎰   in pursuance of the above mentioned
Ordinance, I. [   ] do order that *A.B.*, of   ,
be subject to a periodical Medical Examination by the Visiting Surgeon for
               Months from this Day, for the purpose of ascertaining at the
Time of each such Examination whether she is affected with a Contagious
Disease within the Meaning of the said Ordinance, and that she do attend
for the First Examination at   on the   Day of
               at   o'clock in the   noon.

                                        (Signed.) ———————,
                                                      Registrar General.

————

(F.)

(Voluntary Submission to Examination.)

"THE CONTAGIOUS DISEASES ORDINANCE, 1867."

I, *A.B.*, of   , in pursuance of the above mentioned
Ordinance, by this Submission, voluntarily subject myself to a periodical
Medical Examination by a Visiting Surgeon for   Months
from the Date hereof.

Dated this   Day of   18   .
     Witness,
                                        (Signed,)   A.B.
          X.Y.,
Registrar General.

————

(G.)

(Notice by Visiting Surgeon to Woman of Times, &c., of Examination.)

"THE CONTAGIOUS DISEASES ORDINANCE. 1867."

To *A.B.* of

Take Notice, that in pursuance of the above mentioned Ordinance, you
are required to attend for Medical Examination as follows :

[*Here State Times and Places of Examination.*]

Dated this   Day of   18   .

                                        (Signed,)   E.F.,
                                                      Visiting Surgeon.

(H.)

(Certificate of Visiting Surgeon.)

"THE CONTAGIOUS DISEASES ORDINANCE, 1867."

In pursuance of the above mentioned Ordinance, I hereby certify that I have this Day examined *A.B.* of ...., and that she is affected with a Contagious Disease within the Meaning of that Ordinance; and the Hospital in which she is to be placed under the said Ordinance is the

Dated this .... Day of .... 18 .

(Signed.) E.F.,

Visiting Surgeon.

———

(J.)

(Order by Inspector of Hospitals for Transfer.)

"THE CONTAGIOUS DISEASES ORDINANCE. 1867."

By virtue of the Power in this Behalf vested in me by the above mentioned Ordinance. I hereby order that *A.B.* of ...., now detained under that Ordinance in the Hospital of .... for Medical Treatment, be transferred thence to the Hospital of

Dated this .... Day of .... 18 .

(Signed,) M.N.,

Inspector of Hospitals.

———

(K.)

(Certificate for Detention beyond Three Months.)

"THE CONTAGIOUS DISEASES ORDINANCE, 1867."

I, the undersigned, hereby certify that the further Detention for Medical Treatment of *A.B.* of ...., now an Inmate of this Hospital. is requisite.

Dated this .... Day of .... 18 , at the Hospital.

(Signed,) M.N.,

Visiting Surgeon.

———

(L)

(Discharge from Hospital.)

"THE CONTAGIOUS DISEASES ORDINANCE, 1867."

In pursuance of the above mentioned Ordinance, I hereby discharge *A.B.* of ...., from this Hospital [add according to the Fact,] and certify that she is now free from a Contagious Disease.

Dated this .... Day of .... 18 , at the Hospital.

(Signed.) G.H.,

Visiting Surgeon.

(M.)

(Certificate on Discharge from Imprisonment.)

"THE CONTAGIOUS DISEASES ORDINANCE, 1867."

Whereas under the above mentioned Ordinance *A.B.* of
was on the   Day of   convicted of the Offence of
and has since been imprisoned for that Offence in
and is now discharged from Imprisonment
therein: Now in pursuance of the said Ordinance I hereby certify that she
is now free from a Contagious Disease.

Dated this   Day of   18   .

(Signed.)   R.O.,
Visiting Surgeon.

(N.)

(Notice to Woman leaving Hospital.)

"THE CONTAGIOUS DISEASES ORDINANCE, 1867."

To *A.B.*
As you are now leaving this Hospital, I hereby, in pursuance of the above
mentioned Ordinance, give you Notice that you are still affected with a
Contagious Disease.

Dated this   Day of   18   .

(Signed,)   G.H.,
Visiting Surgeon.

Note.—The above mentioned Ordinance provides as follows :—
If on any Woman leaving a Hospital a Notice [*set out Section of Ordinance.*]

(O.)

(Certificate on last foregoing Notice or Copy.)

"THE CONTAGIOUS DISEASES ORDINANCE, 1867."

In pursuance of the within mentioned Ordinance, I hereby certify that
the within named woman is now free from a Contagious Disease.

Dated this   Day of   18   .

(Signed,)   E.F.,
Visiting Surgeon.

(P.)

(Application to be relieved from Examinations.)

"THE CONTAGIOUS DISEASES ORDINANCE, 1867."

To *L.M.*, Esq., Registrar General.

I, *A.B.* of   , being in pursuance of the above mentioned
Ordinance, subject to a periodical Medical Examination on my own Submis-
sion *or under your Order, as the case may be*], dated the
Day of   , do hereby apply to be relieved therefrom.

Dated this   Day of   18   .

(Signed,)   A.B.

Witness, *G.W.*

(Q.)

" THE CONTAGIOUS DISEASES ORDINANCE, 1867."

It is hereby notified that the House [or part of a House] hereinafter mentioned that is to say [describe the same] was on the
Day of   18   , pursuant to Section XXIII. of the above Ordinance, declared by me under my Hand and Seal of Office to be an Unlicensed Brothel.

———————,

Registrar General.

———

(R.)

(Certificate of Hospital Charges.)

"THE CONTAGIOUS DISEASES ORDINANCE, 1867."

In pursuance of the above mentioned Ordinance, I do hereby certify that   of Licensed Brothel No.   has been an Inmate of Certified
Hospital of [   ] from the   Day of
        to the   Day of   , and that the charges hereto marked *A*. are in accordance with the scale of charges fixed by me with the approval of His Excellency the Governor pursuant to Section XLI. of the above mentioned Ordinance.

Dated this   Day of   18   .

——— ———,

Inspector of Hospitals.

APPENDIX (E).

MR. KESWICK'S DISSENT FROM THE REPORT OF THE HONG KONG COMMISSIONERS.

Sir Michael Hicks Beach wrote to Governor Hennessey (on July 9, 1879), requesting an explanation upon this point. At the end of the Report it is stated that

"As Mr. Keswick was about to leave for England," (before the examination of witnesses was concluded) "the evidence already taken was fully discussed, and resolutions were drafted by the Chairman upon the conclusions arrived at. These resolutions were discussed *seriatim*, and, after being modified in certain points, it was agreed that they should form as far as possible, the basis of the report; the examination of witnesses to be continued by the Chairman and Dr. Eitel respecting points not sufficiently cleared up." Sir M. H. Beach adds: . . . "The inference naturally to be drawn from the above is that Mr. Keswick was substantially at one with his fellow Commissioners as to the report. In the spare copies, however, which reached this office on the 5th and 27th of May, I find a note by Mr. Keswick, dated 27th March, ten days subsequent to the date of your despatch under acknowledgment, expressing his dissent from several of the conclusions arrived at by his colleagues."

. . .

Governor Henessey replied to the above in a letter addressed to Sir M. H. Beach's successor, Lord Kimberley, on June 21, 1880, saying:—

". . . Unfortunately Mr. Keswick was absent from Hong Kong when the majority of the witnesses, including the medical officers of the colony and the head of the police were examined, and when the records of the department that had administered the brothel laws were under consideration. He was in England for some time, and on his return to Hong Kong he was unable to deal with the subject as he was summoned to Japan. . . . It will be seen from Dr. Eitel's report that Mr. Keswick's brother Commissioners are of opinion that Mr. Keswick's note is not consistent with the resolutions to which it is alleged he agreed before his departure for England. . . . For this and other reasons I did not think it necessary to notice his opinion that 'the very serious abuses which were proved' were inevitable."

The Report by Dr. Eitel, to which Governor Hennessey alludes, is as follows:—

"I have the honour to submit a brief statement of facts which will in itself afford a sufficient explanation of the discrepancy observed between the note appended to the Contagious Diseases Report by Mr. Keswick and the statements made in the Appendix to the Report (732).

"On the 8th January, 1878, a paper containing a series of draft resolutions intended to form the basis of our Report, was *seriatim* discussed by the three Commissioners, Mr. Keswick, Mr. Hayllar and myself. Many of these draft resolutions had, in consequence of previous discussion (5th January, 1879 *) been specially altered to meet the respective views of

---

* Obviously an error in date. This should be, we apprehend, 5th January, 1878

the individual members of the Commission, and some had, accordingly, been specially altered to meet Mr. Keswick's personal views. The resolutions thus revised *were then signed by all the members of the Commission,* Mr. Keswick adding to his signature words to the effect that the resolutions fairly embody his views on the subject.

"The Report was accordingly drawn up by Mr. Hayllar and myself *in strict accordance with the spirit and letter of the resolutions agreed upon,* and was in type on 1st December, 1878, when a few copies of the Report and Appendix were struck off preparatory to final typographical revision by the Commissioners. Mr. Keswick had returned to Hong Kong, and Mr. Hayllar, with myself, believed and assured his Excellency the Governor that the Report as it stood, barring trifling corrections of typographical errors, would be formally signed by the three members of the Commission without any dissentient note." . . . "A copy of the complete first edition of the Report and Appendix was sent to Mr. Keswick early in December, 1878, and Mr. Hayllar also sent him the paper containing the Resolutions agreed to on 8th January, 1878; but on 25th December, 1878, a conflagration broke out in Hong Kong which destroyed the type, and as this necessitated setting the Report up afresh from the copies previously struck off, a delay of several months occurred.

"By March 1st, 1879, the second edition of the Report, identically the same as the first, was finished. . . . I called on Mr. Keswick on March 26th, 1879, but was surprised to find that he declined signing the Report.

"On my reminding him that he had in January, 1878, agreed to the Resolutions then drawn up, and that the report tallied exactly with those resolutions, he replied that HE HAD SINCE THEN HAD CONVERSATIONS WITH NAVAL AND MILITARY DOCTORS and others, and CHANGED HIS MIND. Remembering then that in the case of the Royal Commission Report, a minority of members of the Commission recorded their divergent views in a memorandum appended to the Report, I suggested to Mr. Keswick to do the same. He accordingly sent me next day the paper headed 'Note by Mr. Keswick,' and signed by himself. This is the note which appears appended to our Report, and to which I added, on the printed proof, the date '27th March, 1879.'

"The Report and Appendix, identically the same as the first edition of December, 1878 (with the exception of the divergent note of Mr. Keswick, now added), was accordingly republished on 27th March, 1879.

"In December, 1879, when my attention was drawn to the fact that Mr. Keswick's divergence of views, and the existence of a double edition of the Report (December, 1878, and March, 1879), had been noticed elsewhere, I communicated with Mr. Hayllar, asking him to let me have the paper containing the resolutions of 8th January, 1878.

"Mr. Hayllar then told me that the paper had been sent by him to Mr. Keswick, in December, 1878, and *had not been returned to him,* and he added that if he had been in the colony when Mr. Keswck appended his note to our report, he would have protested against it as a contravention of our agreement of 8th January, 1878. *The paper has not been found since.*

(Signed) " E. T. EITEL."

APPENDIX. (F).

"BROTHEL SLAVERY."

Lord Kimberley attempts to found upon an extract from Governor Hennessey's despatch of June 15, 1881, a statement, in the form of a quotation, that the women in Chinese houses are "in great dread of their keepers, and have no courage to seek their freedom," the theory that *brothel slavery* exists only in the brothels frequented by the Chinese. The attempt is entirely disengenuous, as the reader will be enabled to infer if he will refer to the despatch itself, given in the text. The Governor was writing to prove that brothel slavery was "*intensified*" by Ordinance 12 of 1857, and that Ordinance 10 of 1867 "by giving larger powers to the Registrar-General, and thereby, indirectly, to the inspectors with whom the practical working of the Ordinance lies. made the condition of the unfortunate women sold into slavery *worse* than before." Reference to the despatch will show that the "extraordinary dread" entertained by the women conveyed into the Colony is, a dread of all *foreigners ;* and that they fear their keepers because those keepers "look upon the inspectors"—the foreigners —"as their proctectors ;" that the "licensing of the brothels gives the keepers a sort of *official* authority" (derived from the dreaded foreigners) because the keepers "boast of the protection of the inspectors" and that the "natural consequence" of this interference of the foreigners and of the threat of the horrible examination enforced by the foreigners is, that the women "have no courage to seek their freedom."

Equally disengenuous is Lord Kimberley's use of Mr. Cecil C. Smith's assertion that "these instances of virtual slavery exist only in the brothels for Chinese." Mr. C. C. Smith is speaking of the species of slavery which Mr. Labouchere desired to mitigate, the "buying and selling of women for purposes of prostitution," not of the still more grievous moral slavery produced by intensifying that evil through the official protection afforded to their purchasers, by the Contagious Diseases Ordinances.

Mr. Smith says : (Doc. 75 referring to the working of Ordinance 12 of 1867. Appendix to report, Hong Kong Commissioners, page 254).

"Yet while these cases and others having the wilful commission of an offence for a foundation, give rise to the assertion that a system of virtual slavery exists in the brothels in Hong Kong, they are, in my opinion happily very exceptional, compared with what I understand was brought to light in former years. Buying and selling still takes place, but of the two (or it may be three parties to the transaction), each is a willing participator as a rule, or if she who is most concerned proves unwilling, she either does not care or dare to give the necessary evidence for the law to take effect."

From this " buying and selling " the women have been set free by law, and the evidence before the Commission shows that the women who do avail themselves of their right to leave the brothels at their pleasure are precisely the women in the brothels for Chinese.

Inspector Whitehead told the Commissioners (answer 345) " women rarely go from foreign to Chinese brothels " and (346) "in the Chinese brothels there is much fluctuation. Every morning there are ' from 20 to 30 changes, sometimes 50 including changes in servants.' " And Mr. C. C. Smith who told the Commissioners (answer 6) that " many of the women contract a debt with the brothel-keepers and then work it off," adds : (answer 12) " *all the inmates in the brothels know that they are free*, but the national custom is very strong against their leaving them " (the brothels) " in debt." And (answer 10) " the inmates consider their debts to the brothel-keepers to be debts of honour, at least they honestly attempt to pay them off by their earnings."

It is precisely this fact that the inmates of the brothels know that they are legally free, that explains Governor Hennessey's assertion that the Brothel Ordinances have *rendered their condition worse*. Those who are dissatisfied are prevented from leaving by the threat of being conveyed by the Inspectors to examination by the dreaded foreign doctors, and if, rightly or wrongly, pronounced diseased, to imprisonment in the Lock hospital. This is the system of terror, by which, although Lord Kimberley chooses to ignore it—the condition of the unhappy women is intensified into a *real* slavery of a most hideous kind.

In all other respects every witness, from Mr. Cecil C. Smith downwards, gives evidence to show that the women are far better off in Chinese brothels than in the brothels registered for foreigners.

Mr. Smith writes to the Under-Secretary of State for the Colonies, January 18, 1869 (Appendix Report, p. 253):—

"There can be no doubt that the inmates of the brothels licensed for Europeans are of the lowest class to be found in the Colony, who have in most instances found in such a trade the only hope of gaining a livelihood. Their ranks are with difficulty recruited," &c.

And of the brothels for Chinese he says :—

" The inmates of a large number of these are of a far better class than can be found in the other houses. In some cases indeed they are not there primarily for the purposes of prostitution, but simply that they may assist in making the numerous entertainments given in the brothels attractive through their musical accomplishments. These women are not unfrequently bought or redeemed out of the brothel by rich merchants who ultimately take them home as a second and third wife. This buying however is, I believe, no more than following out the principle which obtains in China of the future husband paying money to his father or mother-in-

law as a dowry when he takes his bride to his own house. It is, nevertheless, among such women that it would be impracticable to introduce a
system of medical inspection. They would consider that the interference
of the foreigner in such a matter would cause them to lose caste, and they
would decline to remain in houses subject to such supervision. And in this
they would be followed by the less respectable (if I may use the term
when speaking of these persons) of their number, who, however degraded
they may be, still preserve all the prejudices and superstitious feelings of
their class. They look upon the Lock Hospital as worse than a prison . . ."

Inspector Lee also told the Commissioners (Ans. 456 and
457) :—

" In the brothels for Chinese the women are of a higher class than in
those for Europeans ; (457) second-class prostitutes for Chinese are equal to
the first-class for Europeans. I arrive at this conclusion from inspection."

APPENDIX (G).

Mr. Alfred Lister, Registrar General, told the Commissioners,
Ans. 114, " On the whole I preferred that an informer if he went
to a brothel at all, should be able to state that he had had connexion with a woman, as I thought it very unjust that a woman
should be condemned simply because she had a dollar in her possession."

tho individual members of the Commission, and some had, accordingly, been specially altered to meet Mr. Keswick's personal views. The resolutions thus revised *were then signed by all the members of the Commission,* Mr. Keswick adding to his signature words to the effect that the resolutions fairly embody his views on the subject.

"The Report was accordingly drawn up by Mr. Hayllar and myself *in strict accordance with the spirit and letter of the resolutions agreed upon,* and was in type on 1st December, 1878, when a few copies of the Report and Appendix were struck off preparatory to final typographical revision by the Commissioners. Mr. Keswick had returned to Hong Kong, and Mr. Hayllar, with myself, believed and assured his Excellency the Governor that the Report as it stood, barring trifling corrections of typographical errors, would be formally signed by the three members of the Commission without any dissentient note." . . . "A copy of the complete first edition of the Report and Appendix was sent to Mr. Keswick early in December, 1878, and Mr. Hayllar also sent him the paper containing the Resolutions agreed to on 8th January, 1878; but on 25th December, 1878, a conflagration broke out in Hong Kong which destroyed the type, and as this necessitated setting the Report up afresh from the copies previously struck off, a delay of several months occurred.

"By March 1st, 1879, the second edition of the Report, identically the same as the first, was finished. . . . I called on Mr. Keswick on March 26th, 1879, but was surprised to find that he declined signing the Report.

"On my reminding him that he had in January, 1878, agreed to the Resolutions then drawn up, and that the report tallied exactly with those resolutions, he replied that HE HAD SINCE THEN HAD CONVERSATIONS WITH NAVAL AND MILITARY DOCTORS and others, and CHANGED HIS MIND. Remembering then that in the case of the Royal Commission Report, a minority of members of the Commission recorded their divergent views in a memorandum appended to the Report, I suggested to Mr. Keswick to do the same. He accordingly sent me next day the paper headed 'Note by Mr. Keswick,' and signed by himself. This is the note which appears appended to our Report, and to which I added, on the printed proof, the date '27th March, 1879.'

"The Report and Appendix, identically the same as the first edition of December, 1878 (with the exception of the divergent note of Mr. Keswick, now added), was accordingly republished on 27th March, 1879.

"In December, 1879, when my attention was drawn to the fact that Mr. Keswick's divergence of views, and the existence of a double edition of the Report (December, 1878, and March, 1879), had been noticed elsewhere, I communicated with Mr. Hayllar, asking him to let me have the paper containing the resolutions of 8th January, 1878.

"Mr. Hayllar then told me that the paper had been sent by him to Mr. Keswick, in December, 1878, and *had not been returned to him,* and he added that if he had been in the colony when Mr. Keswek appended his note to our report, he would have protested against it as a contravention of our agreement of 8th January, 1878. *The paper has not been found since.*

(Signed) "E. T. EITEL."

APPENDIX. (F).

"BROTHEL SLAVERY."

Lord Kimberley attempts to found upon an extract from Governor Hennessey's despatch of June 15, 1881, a statement, in the form of a quotation, that the women in Chinese houses are "in great dread of their keepers, and have no courage to seek their freedom," the theory that *brothel slavery* exists only in the brothels frequented by the Chinese. The attempt is entirely disengenuous, as the reader will be enabled to infer if he will refer to the despatch itself, given in the text. The Governor was writing to prove that brothel slavery was "*intensified*" by Ordinance 12 of 1857, and that Ordinance 10 of 1867 "by giving larger powers to the Registrar-General, and thereby, indirectly, to the inspectors with whom the practical working of the Ordinance lies, made the condition of the unfortunate women sold into slavery *worse* than before." Reference to the despatch will show that the "extraordinary dread" entertained by the women conveyed into the Colony is, a dread of all *foreigners ;* and that they fear their keepers because those keepers "look upon the inspectors"—the foreigners—"as their proctectors ;" that the "licensing of the brothels gives the keepers a sort of *official* authority" (derived from the dreaded foreigners) because the keepers "boast of the protection of the inspectors" and that the "natural consequence" of this interference of the foreigners and of the threat of the horrible examination enforced by the foreigners is, that the women "have no courage to seek their freedom."

Equally disengenuous is Lord Kimberley's use of Mr. Cecil C. Smith's assertion that "these instances of virtual slavery exist only in the brothels for Chinese." Mr. C. C. Smith is speaking of the species of slavery which Mr. Labouchere desired to mitigate, the "buying and selling of women for purposes of prostitution," not of the still more grievous moral slavery produced by intensifying that evil through the official protection afforded to their purchasers, by the Contagious Diseases Ordinances.

Mr. Smith says : (Doc. 75 referring to the working of Ordinance 12 of 1867. Appendix to report, Hong Kong Commissioners, page 254).

"Yet while these cases and others having the wilful commission of an offence for a foundation, give rise to the assertion that a system of virtual slavery exists in the brothels in Hong Kong, they are, in my opinion happily very exceptional, compared with what I understand was brought to light in former years. Buying and selling still takes place, but of the two (or it may be three parties to the transaction), each is a willing participator as a rule, or if she who is most concerned proves-unwilling, she either does not care or dare to give the necessary evidence for the law to take effect."

From this " buying and selling " the women have been set free by law, and the evidence before the Commission shows that the women who do avail themselves of their right to leave the brothels at their pleasure are precisely the women in the brothels for Chinese.

Inspector Whitehead told the Commissioners (answer 345) " women rarely go from foreign to Chinese brothels " and (346) " in the Chinese brothels there is much fluctuation.   Every morning there are ' from 20 to 30 changes. sometimes 50 including changes in servants.' "   And Mr. C. C. Smith who told the Commissioners (answer 6) that " many of the women contract a debt with the brothel-keepers and then work it off," adds : (answer 12) " all the inmates in the brothels know that they are free, but the national custom is very strong against their leaving them " (the brothels) " in debt."   And (answer 10) " the inmates consider their debts to the brothel-keepers to be debts of honour, at least they honestly attempt to pay them off by their earnings."

It is precisely this fact that the inmates of the brothels know that they are legally free, that explains Governor Hennessey's assertion that the Brothel Ordinances have rendered their condition worse. Those who are dissatisfied are prevented from leaving by the threat of being conveyed by the Inspectors to examination by the dreaded foreign doctors, and if, rightly or wrongly, pronounced diseased, to imprisonment in the Lock hospital.   This is the system of terror, by which, although Lord Kimberley chooses to ignore it—the condition of the unhappy women is intensified into a real slavery of a most hideous kind.

In all other respects every witness, from Mr. Cecil C. Smith downwards, gives evidence to show that the women are far better off in Chinese brothels than in the brothels registered for foreigners.

Mr. Smith writes to the Under-Secretary of State for the Colonies, January 18, 1869 (Appendix Report, p. 253) :—

"There can be no doubt that the inmates of the brothels licensed for Europeans are of the lowest class to be found in the Colony, who have in most instances found in such a trade the only hope of gaining a livelihood. Their ranks are with difficulty recruited," &c.

And of the brothels for Chinese he says :—

" The inmates of a large number of these are of a far better class than can be found in the other houses.   In some cases indeed they are not there primarily for the purposes of prostitution, but simply that they may assist in making the numerous entertainments given in the brothels attractive through their musical accomplishments.   These women are not unfrequently bought or redeemed out of the brothel by rich merchants who ultimately take them home as a second and third wife.   This buying however is, I believe, no more than following out the principle which obtains in China of the future husband paying money to his father or mother-in-